Ever Faithful, Ever Loyal

The Timothy Alexander Story

Timothy Alexander & Tim Stephens

ISBN Number: 978-0-9858021-7-2

Library of Congress Number: Pending

To Contact Author Timothy Alexander
Email: InspiredbyTA@gmail.com
Website: www.inspiredbyTA.com

To Contact Author Tim Stephens:
Email: tim@timstephensmedia.com
Phone: 954-873-0325
Website: www.timstephensmedia.com

To Contact Hilltop30 Publishers, LLC:
Tom Brew, President & Editor
P.O. Box 973 ** Schererville, Indiana 46375
Email: tombrew@hilltop30.com
Phone: (727) 412-4008
Website: www.hilltop30.com

DEDICATION

I dedicate this book to my Mom and my brother, David. My hero! Thank you for never giving up on me even when there were times you needed to because I was causing so much hell. Although you thought there was nothing you could do with me, you stuck by my side and somehow saw the best in me!

David, your last words to me before you were called to heaven were to "make something out of yourself, Tim, and do something for Ma and the family."

Well, that time has come! This is for you and Ma.

– Timothy Alexander

To Mom and Dad. Thanks for your unending support.
When I was a little boy, you encouraged me
to write and to chase my dreams.
You told me I'd write a book someday.
This is for you.

– Tim Stephens

TABLE OF CONTENTS

TABLE OF CONTENTS *(cont.)*

FOREWARDS

By Dr. Tim Elmore
President, Growing Leaders

When you meet Timothy Alexander, you don't forget him.

He is unique in many ways, and for a variety of reasons. If you were to watch him play high school football in Alabama years ago, you'd be convinced you were going to see him play in the NCAA one day, and probably the NFL. He was tall, and built strong. When he carried the ball, it often took more than one tackler to stop him.

Since his tragic accident in 2006, everyone began to see that Timothy is bigger on the inside than he is on the outside. In the car wreck, he suffered brain injuries and was paralyzed from the waist down—but that has not stopped this man from continuing to make progress in impacting the world.

Dr. Tim Elmore

I remember first meeting Timothy at an athletic forum we hosted at Growing Leaders a few years ago. He rolled into the room in a wheelchair and, without trying, he took over the room. Without a hint of regret, depression or hopelessness, he interacted with people as though the accident was part of his life plan. He still lives "on mission" and continues to leave a positive mark on everyone he meets.

When I met him, I soon began to feel that I was the one who was handicapped. Why? Because with only half of his body functioning, he does more than I do to lift the spirits of those he meets. He gives them encouragement and direction, offers them a sense of vision for their future, and instills the belief that they can do anything. With half a body, he does what I can only attempt to do with a full body.

Timothy is a picture of resilience. I've watched him get in and out of cars, hop in his wheelchair without help, grab the bags he'll need for his next event, and never once complain that it takes twice the time and effort it would for a healthy person. I find myself gaining perspective on my own life when I'm with him. I get an attitude adjustment. I suddenly remember what really matters in life and how life itself is both fragile and unforgiving. Things can go wrong. Big time. Timothy, however, just seems to know how to stay in the "driver's seat" in the midst of tough circumstances, rather than be a "passenger" in life, playing the victim card to excuse himself from hard work or excellence. He believes the accident was just a detour on how he's going to reach his goal. To quote one of our Habitudes®, he believes tough times are *tollbooths not roadblocks.*

So what have I learned most from him?

First, *Timothy is relational.* He genuinely cares about those he meets and the people he has placed in his inner circle. He loves deeply and authentically. No accident has been able to take that away from him. People matter to him. His faith matters to him. Those are qualities that purposeful people grasp.

Second, *Timothy is resourceful.* His accident took some tools away from him, like how his brain functions and how his legs and feet function. But he makes up for what he lacks by making the most of what he has left. One reason I love Timothy Alexander is that he leverages the abilities he still has left rather than complain about what he has lost.

Third, as I mentioned earlier, *Timothy is resilient*. In our world today, this is a meta-competency. His ability to bounce back and continue forging ahead inspires me. The ridiculous rigor he displays in rehab, and the commitment to set and reach goals takes all my excuses away for not hitting my own targets. Like the Energizer Bunny, he just keeps going.

So, I will say it again. Timothy Alexander is a unique individual. I hope you enjoy reading this book and gleaning the lessons I have by watching his life. You will see his uniqueness and likely conclude as I have — it is sad that this man is unique. The world could use a million more Timothy Alexanders.

By Rachel Baribeau
Host, Sirius XM College Sports Nation
and columnist for GridironNow.com

There are some people that when you meet them, you know your life will be irrevocably different because of their mere presence. Such is the case with Timothy Alexander. He can't help but spread goodness, hope, love and faith wherever he goes. It is who he is at his core.

I will never forget watching my team (the Sons of UAB alumni football players) come together to push him across the goal line at the spring game in 2015, when the football program's future was unknown at UAB. He scored the winning touchdown. I ran out onto the field toward him with tears streaming down my face, toward that ray of sunshine, the walking miracle that is Timothy Alexander. To him I'm simply "Coach," because I was fortunate enough to coach him for two straight years—and two straight wins, I might add—when UAB football was in limbo and then reinstated.

He has come to me over the years for advice, prayer, to seek media training, etc., but every single time, I find the roles reversed. He is the teacher and I am the student. I soak him in, his exuberant smile, his contagious spirit, his unparalleled passion for UAB and everyone he comes into contact with on a daily basis. There is no halfway for Timothy Alexander. Whether it's his desire to walk again, his faith, family, UAB football, or anyone else that is fortunate to come into contact with him, he will fight relentlessly for you. You know that from almost the instant you meet him.

Rachel Baribeau

He is that powerful.

People like Timothy don't just change their environment, they don't just change their neighborhood, and that would be amazing in itself. No, people like Timothy set the world on fire with their good deeds. They change the narrative on a grand scale. The world is a better place because of Timothy Alexander and I am fortunate to call him a friend.

By Lauren Sisler, Multimedia reporter for Alabama Media Group and reporter for SEC Nation on the SEC Network

If there is someone in this world who will defy the odds, turn every "no" into a "yes," every "can't" into an "I will," it's Timothy Alexander. I had the honor of meeting Timothy at a UAB baseball game one spring afternoon in 2012. As a local sports reporter, Timothy asked me if I would take a picture with him. Little did I know that was the start of a very special relationship that has had a tremendous impact on my life and something for which I will always be grateful.

Lauren Sisler

More than a year passed before Timothy and I would cross paths again. It was a hot summer day in August 2013 and I can still hear Timothy calling my name from the sidelines of Legion Field. "Hey Lauren, remember me? I'm Timothy Alexander and I'm on the UAB football team now." When I turned around and looked into Timothy's eyes, something inside me knew this young man had an incredible story just waiting to be shared with the world.

As a sports journalist based in the state of Alabama, I've had my share of covering a multitude of sports and events from college football to NASCAR to professional golf. I've traveled all over the country following the Alabama Crimson Tide and Auburn Tigers on their national championship runs. I witnessed the rise, fall, and resurrection of the UAB football program. I've even had the honor of interviewing some of most prolific coaches and athletes in sports. But I always circle back and reflect on Timothy Alexander's story. His story is a reminder to me that victories in life are far greater than those that happen on the playing field when the clock hits zero.

Everybody plays to win, but it's how we overcome and learn from our losses that really help define our success. Timothy lost his ability to walk—and if it's up to him, only temporarily—and yet he shows people how to walk through life every day with undeniable strength, confidence, and faith in God.

To my brother Timothy Alexander, I love you.

1

Chapter

Doomsday

Timothy Alexander raced down University Boulevard, stopping at each building to spread the message, classroom to classroom. "We've got to save UAB football! We need you at the Administration Building!" he shouted. Students followed, with the blessings of their professors. The marchers filled the street outside the office of the president of the University of Alabama at Birmingham. UAB football player Timothy Alexander, fist defiantly in the air, led the chants:

"Free UAB! Free UAB! Free UAB!"

"Save UAB football! Save UAB football!"

A few hours later, Timothy sat in the front row as more than 120 young men and their coaches gathered inside a dank meeting room a few blocks away. The hastily-called gathering had actually been clandestinely planned for months, but it seemed so sudden for members of the UAB football team.

On Dec. 2, 2014, they were just three days removed from 45-24 victory over rival Southern Mississippi that had concluded UAB's regular season with a 6-6 record. It secured bowl eligibility for the long-suffering Blazers for the first time in a decade.

At any other NCAA Division I university, a team meeting on the ensuing Tuesday likely would be to accept a bowl bid, a celebration of a program on the upswing that had experienced one of the best turnarounds in college football in 2014. But this meeting was, as first-year head coach Bill Clark described it at the time, "like a funeral."

Or an execution.

UAB Football: 1991-2014.

Rest in pieces.

*** *** ***

At the front of the room – a former lawn-maintenance storage shed converted into a makeshift meeting and locker room more befitting a Pop Warner club than an NCAA Division I football team – stood one of the highest-paid university presidents in the nation with a reported annual salary of more than $853,000. Dr. Ray Watts, neurologist by trade and administrator by decree of the University of Alabama System Board of Trustees, coldly laid out the facts as if he were delivering news of terminal brain cancer to a dying patient.

His first words: UAB football was, as of this meeting, no more. Over. Dead. Watts cited a university-funded strategic review of the athletics department that found the finances were not sustainable, the program didn't have the resources to be successful, and would require millions of dollars in investment just to maintain status quo. As of this dreary afternoon, those on scholarship would be free to find another university to attend.

The university would treat those who opted to stay with class and pay for their education, Watts said, citing talking points the public later would learn had been crafted months in advance by a high-priced crisis management firm from New York.

There were sobs, and groans of disgust. Outside the doors, a throng of angry program supporters —many of them having marched alongside Timothy Alexander before arriving here—filled a parking lot and lined the street, jeering as news bulletins and social media posts began to fill their phones with the dreaded news.

Watts, in only his second year as UAB's president, fielded questions and then a few Blazers took their turns to speak. Among them was former UAB football player Justin Craft, a local business executive and program booster. Craft had spearheaded efforts to raise money in the weeks leading up to the season finale as rumors swirled that the program might be in jeopardy, despite its recent success on the field. As Craft tried to state that he had secured $2 million in pledges and could get much more, Watts cut him off.

"Justin, you don't know what you don't know," Watts said.

UAB kicker Ty Long, a senior who had been with the program through two coaching changes, dozens of losses and countless injuries to players that were blamed in part on the subpar facilities that had never been significantly improved in 25 years, spoke next.

"You're making the worst decision of your life," Long said, a mix of shock and anger dripping through his words. "I don't know how you're going to sleep with this, bro."

As Long talked, Watts cut him off, too.

"We will honor everyone's scholarship," Watts said, pointing a blue water bottle at the players for emphasis. "I understand there is a lot of passion and emotion. So do I have that same passion and emotion. … We want to make this transition as successful as possible. We're going to make sure that everybody is treated honorably."

"It's bigger than what you think," Long shot back. "It's people. It's family. That's what this is. You should have been a part of it, but you're not."

The room turned silent—and rightfully so—for Blazers senior tight end Tristan Henderson, a 26-year-old Army veteran who served in Iraq before suiting up for UAB. As he spoke, cornerback Jordan Ricks captured the scene on his cell phone in a video that would soon go viral on social mediaoutside those walls.

"I was in a bunker in Iraq," Henderson said. "I watched two of my soldiers walk out and get blown up —two of them, right in front of me. And from that day on, I knew what a brotherhood was. I felt it, felt what it meant to my soul. When I came here, that's what this turned into. That's what this is."

Henderson's voice began to rise, his big hand

pointing an index finger at Watts.

"I don't know what I'm going to do. I've got a wife, a 3-year-old son. My son asked me last night, 'Daddy, what are they going to do with the program?' What am I supposed to explain to him? How am I supposed to look him in the face and tell him? And you're telling me it's because the numbers didn't look right? *The numbers didn't look right?"*

Henderson stood, turning first toward his teammates and then directly at Watts, his 6-foot-4, 265-pound frame casting an imposing figure as he grew more animated with each word.

"You're going to go home, sleep in a comfortable, big-ass house. Dr. Watts, I'm almost 27 years old in a week. Twenty-seven years old. There are 18-year-olds in here, 17-year-olds. What are they supposed to do? Some of these cats came from 3,000 miles away to play here, to be a part of all of this. And you come at us and say numbers? That's what you say?"

Watts' face grew red as players grew restless. He pointed the water bottle at them again.

"You've got a few years at UAB," he lectured. "I've got 42. I came here, I was an undergraduate. I worked my (backside) off ..."

Amid the players' groans at that statement, Long fired a question at the UAB president: "Did (UA System trustee) Paul Bryant Jr. make your decision?"

"Please be quiet!" Watts shot back, angrily pointing that bottle again, his own level of frustration rising by the minute. "If you don't want to be quiet, I'll leave.

... There's nobody in this room, and nobody out there, nobody in this city or state, that cares more about UAB than I do."

The statement was met with immediate groans. A few players stomped out of the room in disgust.

"He was scared," Henderson would say later of Watts. "He's a guy who hasn't been in this position before, and he is in front of 120 people who are absolutely (furious).

"One of the top reasons is that we have never seen him. We have never heard from him. I have never seen this guy anywhere we have ever been. I have never even seen him at the school. So for him to come out and say 'yeah, I am your number one fan,' — OK, now you are lying. That was the reaction."

Photo courtesy of Nic Gulas/WIAT42

Surrounded by fans and supporters, Timothy Alexander talks to media after learning that the UAB football, bowling and rifle teams had been terminated by the university on Dec. 2, 2014.

The meeting, obviously, was not going well. The sooner it was over, the better.

"Coach Clark tells him he better leave, that things are about to get serious," Henderson recalled. "There is a point where the tension is so high in that room, if Watts didn't leave, those fans would have come inside. That tension was growing in that room, and it was growing outside. He had to go. His neck was on the chopping block and the executioner was on the way up."

With that, Watts gave a wave and was whisked out the back door by armed university police officers, who then weaved him through the gauntlet of angry UAB football fans, his eyes growing wide and his crimson face draining pale as the hundreds who surrounded the building, hurling curse words and raining down boos, turned their anger onto him with signs that they shook like pitchforks and torches.

"Coward!" a man shouted.

As he ducked into a black sports utility vehicle and officers tried to push back the mob, fans pounded on the back windshield. A touch of the gas pedal by his driver, and Watts was gone.

So was UAB football, leaving an eerie silence. In the aftermath remained shock, anger and complete devastation. Men and women cried. Some sat on the street corner with blank looks on their faces, as if they had just emerged from a storm cellar to discover a tornado had demolished their home.

"Hearing him say the words, it was like

slow-motion," said Lee Miller, former Blazers kicker and president of the letterman's club who was in the back of the room. "I couldn't believe he was actually saying the words that he was shutting the program down."

As Watts was on his way to a press conference, where he would explain to the nation why he had chosen to kill the UAB football program as well the university's bowling and rifle teams, players filed out solemnly.

Some cried. Some hugged. Some looked as if they had just experienced the death of a family member.

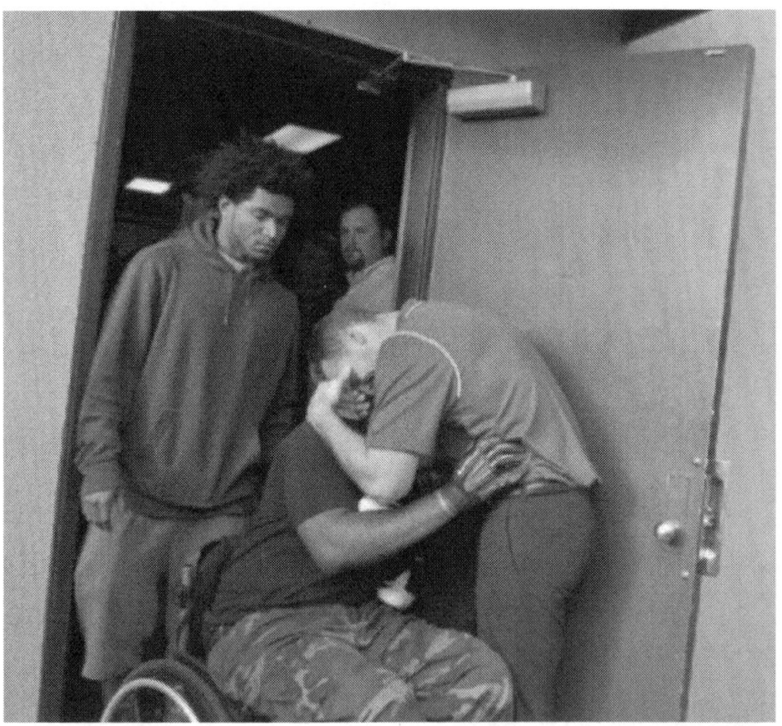

Photo courtesy of Nic Gulas/WIAT42

Timothy Alexander is consoled by UAB strength and conditioning coach Zac Woodfin (right) after learning of the elimination of the Blazers' football program in 2014.

They were greeted by the mob for a collective hug.

"Brutal," is how reporter Jon Solomon, who covered the story for CBSSports.com, described the scene. "I remember taking a picture of two of the players collapsing into the arms of the team chaplain, just crying. It was all so raw."

*** *** ***

UAB football player Timothy Alexander sat in his chair, surrounded by the crowd and the television cameras. In his hands were a special pair of shoes.

"These cleats, man," he said as he held them up, his voice cracking as he tried to hold back tears. "These cleats I wanted to wear at this school. All I want to do is just tell y'all, thank y'all so much. Y'all have been the biggest supporters of our lives, and it means so much to us. These cleats, they go to the students. I don't know who I am going to give them to.

"Continue doing what you are doing," Alexander told the crowd. "We owe you the truth. He said it was all about numbers ..."

"We love you, Tim," voices in the crowd yelled back.

As the next few months would prove, the numbers didn't quite add up. Those who made the decision to shut down the UAB football program miscalculated many things. They underestimated the loyalty inspired by the young head coach, Bill Clark, who infused the program with renewed confidence and commitment.

They underestimated the passion of the fans. They underestimated the resolve of the community and the resources of the business leaders.

But perhaps as much as anything, they underestimated Timothy Alexander, the young man who would rally the community to stand up for the football program—and for itself—in ways no one could have imagined before that dark day in December.

As he clenched his cleats, he made a promise to himself and to those around him that he would never stop fighting for what he believed in. UAB football had given so much to him at a time in his life when he needed hope and opportunity, and he would not let it die without his voice — and the voices of others like him — being heard.

Those who shut down the UAB football, bowling and rifle programs didn't just underestimate Timothy Alexander.

They never saw him coming.

2

Chapter

1st Timothy

Before Timothy Alexander could lead a movement, he first had to find himself. As a teenager growing up in a rough part of Birmingham, Alabama, Timothy Alexander was lost.

Lost, and angry.

Born on December 14, 1988, Timothy grew up in the Center Point area in Jefferson County, just north of Birmingham. He was mostly estranged from his father, Marvin Alexander, and raised by his mother, Patricia, a devoutly religious woman of stout resolve who expected her boys to live right and do right. Timothy had two much-older brothers. Fred was 14 years older than Timothy. He shared a much-closer bond with David, seven years older and still under his mother's roof as Timothy grew into adolescence. As a young child, Timothy was happy-go-lucky, always looking to get a laugh and always flashing a big smile. He got his biggest joys on the football field, a game he fell in love with early in his life, starting with his days in a recreation league at Huffman Park at around age 5, around the same time his parents divorced.

Timothy was a child who loved to smile—and to make others smile. Nowhere did his smile shine more than when there was a football in his hands.

"He loved it," Patricia Alexander said. "He loved playing ball and getting ready for it, being with his teammates. That was the most important part."

"He was passionate about that sport," his uncle, Wayne Woolf, recalled.

But as he grew into a teenager and entered E.B. Erwin High School, Timothy's mood changed. On the surface, friends saw the big smile. Underneath was rage

Photo courtesy of Patricia Alexander

From the time he started playing at age 5, Timothy Alexander found joy in the game of football.

—and it soon wouldn't be contained.

Timothy Alexander was on a dark path to nowhere, and everyone around him was beginning to see it.

"I was angry," Timothy recalled. "Angry at the world."

"He was being very rebellious and disobedient," Patricia said. "If I said it was raining, he was going to argue that no, it was not."

"He was not the perfect son, and in his anger, he was getting into trouble and doing things that he knew were not the way that I had taught him to be."

He often left home for long stretches. He'd get angry about something and leave to run the streets with friends. His mother didn't know where he was, and didn't ask. He was capable of good grades "when he applied himself," but didn't seem interested in school.

"I joined a gang," Timothy said. "I did a lot of things I shouldn't have done."

"It was very heartbreaking to me at that time," Patricia said. "I wanted Timothy to succeed and wanted him to be obedient, and it really bothered me that half the time I didn't even know where he was. He was not coming home. He was not calling me to let me know where he was. I would just pray and ask God to protect him, and cover him and protect him from all harm and danger."

Patricia had reached her limit as her youngest son made poor choices.

"The Lord blessed me," she said. "I didn't lose

any sleep, but I didn't know where he was. I did not call him or look for him. The Lord just gave me a rest and I prayed that the Lord would watch over him that he would come to his senses and get out of that wrong crowd before something terrible happened.

"I didn't want him to end up in jail or hell, as a matter of fact. I wanted him to be doing what was right in the eyesight of the Lord."

As he moved into his teenage years, Timothy found himself attracted to fitting in with friends and aspiring to gain money and material things that were glorified in the media around him.

"He was running with the wrong crowd," Patricia said flatly. "Instead of being a leader, he was being a follower. He was listening to the wrong voices, and that is what led him to trouble and despair."

Timothy's first serious brush with the law almost landed him in prison. He was only 16. One of his friends was accused of a sexual assault at a nearby apartment complex. Timothy had been there that day, and although he had not participated in the crime in any way, he was arrested and charged as an accomplice. "Guilt by association," he called it. If convicted as an adult, Timothy faced significant prison time. With her son locked up in jail, Patricia refused to bail him out. He'd gotten himself into the mess by being disobedient, and she wasn't going to enable it. After his father posted bail, Timothy was transferred to a juvenile detention center until the case went to court.

Eventually, Timothy was cleared and the charges

were dismissed. However, this close call did nothing to change Timothy's behavior.

"It was a horrible time," Patricia said. "Timothy just would not listen, even after this. The same day he got released from juvenile, he went back out in the streets."

"Tim's mom, she was very worried about him during our 10th- and 11th-grade year," recalled Anthony Vasser, one of Timothy's best friends and football teammate at Erwin High School. "He had multiple jobs; he didn't take school seriously because he was more interested in earning a dollar than earning an education. She was so worried about that, but Tim was so big among his peers. Everybody looked forward to being around him because they knew what type of character he was.

"He was always looking for the laugh. He would do whatever to get a laugh. That worried his mom that she knew he had a lot of class clown in him, but she also could see his potential."

***   ***   ***

Trouble found Timothy, and sometimes he found trouble himself.

The bag was just sitting there. Too easy. Too tempting. It was Timothy's first day on the job, working at a McDonald's restaurant not far from his Center Point home.

"I went in there in the back office, and my manager told me to put my book bag down in this room," Timothy recalled. "When I threw it down, my book bag hit the safe and the safe opened up. I was like, 'Oh my gosh.'"

Inside the safe was a bag full of money. Timothy told a co-worker, who was one of his friends, about the safe and the bag of money that was there for the taking. A plan was hatched.

"We decided we were going to take the money and hide it," Timothy said.

Timothy and his friend stuffed the money into the book bag and then hid it outside. They then went about their work, planning to pocket it after their shift. But, of course, management soon noticed the missing cash and called the police. It didn't take them long to find the book bag filled with the McDonald's cash for the day, which led them straight to Timothy and his accomplice.

Soon he was on his way to jail.

"The only thing that saved me from going down into the system and ruining my life was that I was so young, maybe 16," Timothy said. "I had to go on probation. I had to go on house arrest. I was in juvenile (detention) and I saw how the kids were being treated on the inside, the fighting and gang violence and having to do different things—me having to do right. When you are locked away, you get a lot of time to yourself and to think about your life. I was in there maybe two or three months."

***   ***   ***

His first night behind bars was eventful. Even at 16 years old, Timothy was savvy to the culture of violence. When he was placed in a holding cell, he laid down on a cot. Soon came a test of his toughness.

"This guy came up and told me to get off his cot," Timothy remembered. "I got into a fight with him right then and beat him up. I knew I had to stand up for myself or I would get singled out."

From the detention center, he called his mother. Where he expected sympathy, he instead received discipline.

"She was like, 'You did it to get in there; you're going to learn a lesson.' "

Timothy's brother David and his mother came to see him in juvenile lockup. Timothy met them in handcuffs.

His brother tore into him about his behavior — more with his eyes and body language than with words. It stunned Timothy, both in its ferocity and pain. Shame washed over him. David's disappointment with Timothy stung him deeply. David and his other brother, Fred, had never been in trouble. And now here was Timothy, the baby of the family, breaking his mother's heart.

"I saw the tears in my brother's eyes," Timothy recalled. "He just shook his head. I could see the hurt in his eyes. I knew I had really hurt my brother and my mom. I didn't really have a dad at home, so my brother was like my dad. I never wanted to disappoint him.

"I had never seen my brother cry at all. So I was like, 'I've got to get my act together.' "

Soon there would be a meeting with a judge, and a chance to get out of confinement.

"The judge was like, 'What are you going to do if I let you out?' I told her I was going to go to work and I'm going to turn my life around. I told her I had good grades and that I was just surrounding myself with the wrong crowd."

That crowd was unquestionably leading Timothy toward real consequences. He came home with an ankle monitor that tracked his movements. There were more arrests to come, more interactions with law enforcement and the very real possibility that before he turned 17, Timothy might be charged as an adult, perhaps not even for things he personally did, but for being so close to the crimes of others. That was gang life.

"When you are young, your life is going so fast around you," Timothy recalled. "I was focused on the negative influences."

Timothy was at a crossroads, but more trouble was to come.

3

Chapter

His Brother's Keeper

By the time he was a teenager, there were few people Timothy Alexander trusted or respected. Seven years older than Timothy, his brother David could at least get his attention.

"Timothy and David were very close," their mother, Patricia, said.

"We shared everything," Timothy recalled. "We shared a bedroom. We shared a dresser. We shared clothes. Even though I was younger than him, I was bigger than him by the time I was in high school, so I wore his clothes. He used to get so mad at me that he would come to the school and make me take off his clothes."

David played baseball in youth league and was known as quite the pitcher as a kid, but he didn't play sports at Erwin High School.

"He was still the man at Erwin," Timothy recalled. "He ran that school. Everybody liked him. David was more of an outdoors type. He loved to go hunting and fishing. He loved the country and being out in the woods."

Timothy remembers coming home one day to find a freshly killed deer. David had been hunting and now there was work to do.

"David taught me how to skin the deer," Timothy remembered. "He handed me a knife and showed me how to cut off the hide and cut out the guts."

David took great interest in Timothy's love of football. After school, the two would work out in the back yard. David taught Timothy routes, taught him how to catch, taught him how to use his growing body to his advantage against smaller defenders. David pushed Timothy to be his best.

"When I would have a game, no matter what happened, he would always point out things I could do better," Timothy recalled.

The brothers were hyper-competitive, especial-

Photo courtesy of Patricia Alexander

Timothy (right) with his mother Patricia and brothers Fred and David on Fred's wedding day. Timothy was especially close to David (left).

ly as Timothy began to grow into the body that would some day make him a college football prospect. Timothy had little trouble beating the kids his own age in anything athletic, but his brother was another story.

"I couldn't beat him at anything," Timothy recalled. "The only competition I really had was my brother. I always wanted to be better than my brother at everything. My brother was a man's man — a country boy who was rough and tough. I wanted to be better than him."

That competitiveness spilled over into computer games.

"I couldn't even beat him in Madden," Timothy said of the popular NFL computer game. "One time we were playing and I almost won. He turned it off and said the power went out."

The two often would have footraces at his grandmother's house. David always won those, too.

Timothy would put all that training into practice off the field, too. There was a particular yard in the neighborhood that was fenced; behind the chain link were pit bulls. Timothy and a friend would test their speed by teasing those dogs into a frenzy.

"I would sneak over the fence and unlock the latch and bark at the dogs," Timothy said. "The dogs would chase us when we would take off running."

That's one way to get into shape; fear is a good motivator. Did Timothy ever get caught?

"One of those dogs caught me one time and bit me on the back of my leg," he said with a hearty laugh.

As Timothy grew older and bigger, he would challenge David's authority in the house.

"David used to get so mad because I would take his car without permission," Timothy said. "We would get into fist fights."

"Yes, they would fight," Patricia recalled.

Timothy always seemed to push his older brother's limits. And Patricia's, too.

"Sometimes it would get rough and Ma would kick us out of the house, tell us that there wasn't going to be no breaking of her stuff and that if we were going to do that, take it outside," Timothy said with a laugh.

One time in particular, Timothy was getting the upper hand.

"David slipped while we were fighting and I put him in a choke hold and almost choked him out. Later on that night he told a friend, 'I can't try him anymore; he's turned into a man.'"

Timothy laughs now at a picture of the family from older brother Fred's wedding day in 2005. There is David, Patricia and Fred, and then Timothy—with no smile.

"I was mad in that picture because David had taken my jacket. His came back too small and so he took mine," Timothy said.

Despite whatever sibling rivalries there might have been, Timothy held immense respect for his older brother. He would tell David his dreams of playing college football, of making the NFL. Whenever he was on the field, his brother's coaching and encouragement were never far from his mind. David's feedback meant a lot to him at a time when there were not yet many consistent male authority figures in Timothy's life.

"My brother," Timothy said, "he's my hero."

4

Chapter

Tested By Fire

It was a spring Saturday morning in 2006, April Fool's Day. Now a 17-year-old junior at Erwin High, Timothy went to spring football practice, then came home to mow the grass at Patricia's house in Center Point. When he finished, he put the mower in a storage room on the carport and then laid down to take a nap. Normally, Timothy would rinse off the mower before he rolled it into storage, but on this day, tired from practice and not particularly in the mood to do chores, he didn't.

"I was so tired, I literally went inside and fell asleep in the floor," Timothy recalled.

Inside the home, Patricia was reading the Bible, preparing for the Sunday School lesson she was to teach the next morning. The trials of Job, it was. Outside, his brother David was looking for a lost debit card.

The heat from the mower started a fire. Neighbors noticed, and knocked on the door. Patricia ignored them. "I thought it was children wanting Timothy to come out to play, and I didn't want to be bothered," she recalled.

A neighbor persisted—"she beat down the door," Patricia said—and soon the flames were everywhere, smoke billowing from the house.

"I grabbed my robe and my purse and I ran out the door," she said. "Someone says 'fire,' you just take off running."

Timothy still was inside.

"I heard my brother David come in, screaming and shaking me — 'Tim, get up! There's a fire!' " Timothy said. "I'm thinking he is playing. He slapped me to bring me to life, and I see smoke. My brother and I had to run through the front door with our shirts over

Photo courtesy of Patricia Alexander

Older brother, David, and mother, Patricia, tried unsuccessfully to keep a rebellious Timothy out of trouble during his teenage years.

our face to keep from breathing the smoke or getting burned. After we ran out through the driveway, my mother's car caught on fire and David had to get into it and back it out of the driveway.

"The entire home was engulfed in smoke and flames."

The family lost everything.

"Clothes, shoes, everything," Timothy said. "We literally lost everything but the clothes on our backs."

Shockingly, things would get worse.

*** *** ***

It was April 14, 2006. Good Friday. After two weeks in a hotel, Patricia was preparing on this morning to move back into a temporary apartment until the home she owned could be repaired. Friends and church members had raised $5,000 to help the family recover. Timothy came to her hotel room, as he had done every morning during this time.

"We always prayed together before Timothy went to school," Patricia recalled. "That is just how I raised them."

Patricia didn't know David had left. He had driven early that morning to Jacksonville State University, about an hour northeast of Birmingham, where he had been a student. He was there to say goodbye to friends because he had recently decided to transfer to a college in Birmingham. Today, he would return help Patricia move the family into the apartment.

"I didn't know where he was," Patricia said. "I thought maybe he had gone to work. I took Timothy to school and I started getting things ready to move in."

A state trooper had been calling the desk repeatedly, looking for Patricia and leaving several messages. At first, Patricia thought perhaps there was a problem with an insurance check, or maybe friends were playing a prank on her.

Then she thought of Timothy.

"The first thing I said was, 'If Timothy has gotten into trouble again, I am going to beat him.' "

Patricia called her oldest son, Fred, to ask about the strange calls. "I could not put it together why this officer would be looking for me," Patricia said. Fred arrived at the hotel with her grandson. She was outside packing her car when the officer arrived.

He had terrible news.

David had fallen asleep behind the wheel on the drive back from Jacksonville. His car crossed the median on Interstate 20 and hit and 18-wheeler between Birmingham and Anniston, ejecting him from the vehicle.

He died instantly, the officer said. He was 24 years old.

Patricia balled her fist. She pounded on the officer's bullet-proof vest until her screams subsided to sobs. There in the parking lot of a Hampton Inn in Trussville, Alabama, a mother's worst nightmare became her worst reality.

"The house fire, losing my things, I did not care because I knew that the Lord would provide for us,"

Patricia said. "That news about my son, I was just so broken. I lost it."

Fred was dispatched to Erwin High. He checked Timothy out of school and delivered the bad news in the car.

"David's gone," he told Timothy.

The strongest male figure in Timothy's life was taken from him in an instant. They shared a bedroom. They shared clothes. They shared dreams. He was the man Timothy confided in with his aspiration of someday playing in the NFL. He was the man who pushed Timothy to do the right things in school. He was the moral conscience in his ear when other kids around him filled his head with distractions, excuses and opportunities to do the wrong things.

"More or less, my son didn't want Timothy to break my heart," Patricia said of David. "He didn't want me to have to face him in jail or worse. Timothy would look up to David."

Timothy was in complete shock. He cried. He shook. He couldn't speak.

"It was heartbreaking," Patricia said. "Timothy was so pitiful."

"I loved my brother. We were so close," Timothy said.

Unable to cope, Timothy Alexander ran away from what was left of home. He didn't check in with his mother. He didn't comfort her in her grief. He didn't even ride in the family car with his mother to David's funeral.

Patricia was bewildered.

"When I was grieving, I don't know if I was grieving more for David or more for Timothy," she said. "I didn't even know where Timothy was. He never came home. Even the day that we buried David, Timothy didn't come home after the funeral and I didn't even ask where he was going. He was so rebellious. After several days, I called the police and they found him, and that hard head still did not come home. It was a horrible time.

"Sometimes your past will embarrass you, but there is no reason to be embarrassed now. Your brother died in a car accident. Your mother is in an apartment grieving. Our house had just burned and whatever we had was gone. We made it out alive, but you don't have enough love in your heart to stop being with your friends and come home to see about your mother? That hurt me so bad. All I could do was just pray and call out to the Lord."

5

Chapter

A Turning Point

Soon after David's death, Timothy went into a dark depression. Any progress he'd made after his brush with the law was now very much in jeopardy. He needed a jolt, someone or something to replace the voice that David had provided in his head. He found refuge in football, spring practice in 2006 as he was preparing for an upcoming senior year where he hoped to attract the attention of college scouts.

He found direction in the back of a police car.

An argument and physical altercation between Timothy and Patricia brought a messenger that Timothy could hear. Responding to call at Patricia's home, Officer Ali Daniels of the Jefferson County Sheriff's Office was a stern, no-nonsense man who exuded strength and courage.

He found a young man out of control.

"When I came into his presence, he was quite an angry young man," Daniels said. "He was almost combative. I had to take him in to (the) Juvenile (Detention

Center)."

It was a life-changing ride for Timothy.

"Normally, police officers don't talk to you, and I had been in the back of police cars a lot of times," Timothy said. "I grew up very fast.

Photo courtesy of Patricia Alexander

Timothy became a star as a senior tight end at Erwin High School, ranking among the top college prospects in the state. But his dreams of playing college football and making the NFL would end in an instant.

"If it wasn't for Officer Daniels talking to me and showing me that he honestly cared, I think I would have still been in the system. Because he talked to me as a man — and opened his heart up to me as a male figure in a way that I did not have and was longing for—that really helped my life turn around."

Daniels promised Timothy he would stay in contact with him, whether he liked it or not.

"I told him he could talk to me anytime, even after me having to arrest him that particular night," Daniels said. "I held up my end of the deal. I would jump out there periodically and get in touch with him. I let him know that I did care, because I would rather see him change his way of life."

Daniels noticed Timothy's demeanor changed as they talked. "I asked him, 'What do you have to lose by being obedient to your mom?' It's not going to hurt you at all to be obedient to your mother," the officer said. "Try being obedient without the fussing and see how it goes for you and watch how things change. We were talking about trust. Work up that trust and things will begin to change for you. He let me in."

These words would become a theme for Timothy that would change his life in remarkable ways. He began to let people in—or they barged in, whether he was ready for it or not.

*** *** ***

This was the same message Willie Miller had tried to instill in Timothy.

Miller recognized the potential, and when he was promoted from assistant coach to head coach of the Erwin Eagles football team, he wasn't going to watch it go unfulfilled. In his first team meeting in the spring of 2005, he lit into Timothy Alexander, the 6-foot-5, 200-pound junior tight end who had great hands and great speed, but lacked focus and maturity. Timothy hadn't heard anything like that before, especially with such force and passion.

"I had never really had somebody command authority in my life," Timothy recalled.

Like Officer Daniels, Willie Miller could speak to

Timothy in a way he could hear. A hard-nosed Army veteran, he later played seven years in the National Football League with the Cleveland Browns and Los Angeles Rams. He even played in a Super Bowl for the Rams against the Pittsburgh Steelers in 1980.

Miller was no-nonsense all the way. What he saw in Alexander's ability was a potential major-college prospect who was on his way to missing a life-changing opportunity by being immature, unfocused and lazy. He saw Timothy using the big smile to hide from his fears. He saw the bad conduct not as Timothy's inherent nature, but as his way to fit in and gain approval. Beneath that facade, he saw a potential leader with an unrelenting drive to succeed. He saw the leader who would turn around his football program.

Timothy just needed to be challenged, and Miller did that. When the coach asked the entire team who was willing to do the things necessary to be great, Alexander raised his hand. The young man they called "T-Time"—T stood for Touchdown, a nickname he picked up after he scored four touchdowns in the first half of a junior varsity game—got a response he didn't expect.

"Put your hand down, Alexander," the coach groused. "You don't want to be great."

"He jumped me in front of the whole team, called me a clown," Timothy said. "He called me a coward in front of the whole team. He said I was wasting all my ability and that all I cared about was getting laughs and chasing the girls and just getting by in life and that

I wasn't going to work hard."

Anthony Vasser, who played receiver next to Timothy and was one of his best friends at Erwin, remembers how Miller's ambush got the entire team's attention.

"I can remember one night, Coach Miller calling him a coward, because of things he was afraid to attempt. He was so stuck on being among his peers. With those prospects and the type of (college scholarship) offers he was starting to receive, he saw in Tim some things that Tim didn't see in himself. He was looking at small things, and Coach Miller was looking at big things.

"He jumped on him real big in a way that showed how much he cared for Tim. He didn't call him a coward because of what Tim was doing right then. He called him a coward because he was looking at so much bigger than that. He saw the things in Tim and what Tim could be that Tim didn't see him himself. Coach Miller hated that Tim couldn't understand that at the time because Tim just wanted to have fun."

Miller got Timothy's attention by commanding his respect. It was something that had been missing in Timothy's life, having someone who challenged him to achieve and didn't accept anything less than his best. The transformation would be a process, not an overnight change. Despite Miller riding him on the football field, Timothy had not yet gotten his act together off it, leading to the altercation with his mother and that fateful ride with Daniels.

But on the field, potential was being realized, and with that, Timothy began to understand that options were becoming available to him. He quickly became the catalyst for turning around a team that had won only eight of its past 50 games. They won five games in Miller's first season and seemed poised for a run at the playoffs entering Timothy's senior season in the fall of 2006.

Football helped Timothy recapture his smile in the wake of his brother's death. He was the kind of kid who could entertain classmates by donning the school's mascot uniform or cracking a joke that caused a class to laugh. But he also could light up the scoreboard on the football field and excel in the classroom — when he applied himself.

"He had it all," Miller said. "Big, fast, tough, charisma, leadership, talent. Tim was a great athlete. And the thing about Tim, if you got his attention, he was a bulldog. There was absolutely no quit in him. If you told Tim he couldn't do something, he was going to prove you wrong—and he was not going to stop until he did.

"I knew he was going to be our leader and that if I got through to him, the other players would follow his lead and change the direction of the program."

Friends like Vasser marveled at how Alexander could dunk a basketball with ease, or how he was one of the team's best blockers while also being practically uncoverable on passing routes as a tight end.

"He was dominant," Vasser said. "Just

dominant."

*** *** ***

Timothy just needed the grades to go with the athletic ability, and he was quick to admit that he often did just enough in school to get by. That's when another strong man of influence stepped into the picture. Erwin High principal Van Phillips arrived in 2004 to clean up a school ravaged by gangs, drugs, violence and low expectations. "The grad rate when I got there was 49 percent and the dropout rate was over 25 percent," Phillips said. "There had been 84 arrests the year that I came in there and there had been 1,800 office referrals. That is what I walked into."

And his first interactions with Timothy, in 2004, were not good.

"My first impression of Tim was that this boy was not going to live long if he doesn't get himself under control," Phillips said flatly.

"I had to give him some firm discipline," Phillips recalled. "When I was talking to him, it just really hit me in my heart that this young man had an opportunity to be somebody if he could just get out of this fog he was in. He was angry that life had given him a bad deal."

By Timothy's junior year, Phillips was seeing the same things others were seeing.

"He's a tall kid, a nice kid, funny, acts a fool with the fans," Phillips said. "There's a lot to like about him, but he wanted to be a gangbanger. He wanted to be on the wrong side of the law."

Like Miller and Daniels and Timothy's brother before him, Phillips slowly gained Timothy's trust by demanding excellence of him.

He gained that attention in a hard-core way.

"I don't know if I had my hands around his throat," Phillips recalled of the office altercation that turned physical. "I know I definitely had my hands around his shirt. I said, 'Listen here boy, you can either be a gangbanger or a game-changer. You have that much ability in you, if you will just get out of your own way, God will do some special things in your life.

"You need to make a decision TODAY about who you are going to ride with. Are you going to ride with Mr. Phillips or are you going to ride with your gangbangers? But I am telling you right now that Mr. Phillips' team is going to win and I want you to be on my team.' "

Phillips suspended Timothy and sent him briefly to alternative school.

"When he came back, he said, 'Mr. Phillips, I want to be on your team.' "

Timothy's grades improved to match his football prowess, and doors were opening. After a good performance at a summer camp, the letters started to arrive. One scouting service ranked him as one of the top tight end prospects in Alabama and among the state's top-10 prospects overall. Schools like Alabama and Florida were requesting game film. Comparisons were made to another Erwin tight end, Rod Rutledge, who starred at the University of Alabama in the 1990s and later played in the NFL with the New England Patriots.

His NFL dream didn't seem far-fetched, even though his mother always cautioned him to "have a Plan B."

Plan B was not in Timothy's head, however.

"I was going to the NFL, no doubt in my mind," Timothy said.

Others didn't have much doubt either, because he was that special. His teammates still rave about a play he made in a victory over rival Gardendale in 2006.

"Power Wing Right 27 GS," Alexander said, beaming. The play still runs through his mind, years later, where his devastating block wiped out two defenders and cleared the path for the winning touchdown in the final seconds. After the play, he ran to the sidelines and leaped into an assistant coach's arms. "He told me to look up in the stands. 'Tim, you've got coaches here from all over the country watching you. You're going to college.' "

The following week, October 27, they beat Walker High 28-3 to clinch a playoff berth for the first time in seven years. Players stayed out late to celebrate. The next morning, Timothy would take the ACT exam, where a good score was certain to secure major-college opportunities. Life couldn't get much better.

Through it all, memories of his brother David were strong. "He was my motivation," Timothy said. "I dedicated my season to him and I was going to make it to college and the NFL. I was going to change my life and take care of my mom."

It was about to change in an instant.

Chapter

Dreams Demolished

Saturday, October 28, 2006, was supposed to be a day of fun with friends at the Magic City Classic. It was a chance to take his mind off the death of his brother and unwind after a morning of taking the ACT test, where an NCAA-qualifying score would open a world of college football options for Timothy.

Timothy stayed up late celebrating their big football victory, then got up early to take his college entrance exam. The test was a hint that Timothy's priorities still were not in order.

"I was out until about 5:30 a.m., got home and took a power nap and then went to take my ACT," Timothy said. "I was so tired, I didn't even care. I just marked C on all the answers and went to sleep."

He was in no mood for chores when his mother asked him to cut the grass before he and two friends were to go to the game.

"I'll do it when I get back home," he promised. They just had to drop off a friend's child at a relative's house, and then it would be on to Legion Field for the Classic, a college football rivalry between Alabama's two largest historically black universities, Alabama A&M and Alabama State.

Timothy's friend was driving, but he dozed off at the wheel. "We all dozed off," Timothy said. The car careened off the East Lake Park exit ramp on Interstate 59/20 headed toward downtown Birmingham from Center Point.

The car smashed into an overpass guardrail.

The driver and other passengers were unhurt, but Timothy was badly injured. His head was bleeding. Glass covered and cut his body. The car teetered on the edge of the overpass. He broke out the glass of the rear passenger window and pitched the uninjured toddler out to his friends, who had exited the vehicle.

"I saved the baby's life," he said.

But then the car tumbled. Down, down, down, with Timothy in the back seat. The car rolled, over and over, until crashing abruptly into a pole at the bottom of the incline. When officers arrived to survey the wreckage, they initially assumed all passengers were dead because of the extreme damage to the car. They didn't know Timothy's friends and the child had gotten out of the car unharmed.

An ambulance rushed Timothy to UAB Hospital. Erwin High principal Van Phillips was on a golf course when he received a telephone call delivering the bad news. Timothy Alexander, star senior tight end for the Erwin Eagles, was in a terrible accident. One caller said

Timothy was dead.

Phillips wasn't emotionally prepared for what he saw when he arrived at the hospital.

"He looked like death warmed over," Phillips said. "It was the worst I had ever seen anybody."

Tubes and wires extended out of Timothy's body. His face was grossly distorted from the swelling and bruises. He suffered a significant head injury that included brain trauma. His ribs were broken, and there was still a trace of red from where he had coughed up blood. He was bleeding internally. His arms were battered and bruised and immobilized by protective bandaging. He had metal pins in his hands to hold broken bones in place. He was hooked up to machines that kept him alive.

Timothy Alexander was in a coma. He would remain comatose for 10 days and was in the intensive care unit for 20 days. Two days after his accident, while he was unconsciousness, an emergency surgery was performed on his spinal cord in hopes that his movement might be recovered.

"We were in the waiting room for hours," Patricia recalled.

When he finally awoke and was asked about the crash, Timothy said the last thing he remembered of the accident was of someone asking him if he was OK, as smoke began to billow out of the car and arms pulled him from the wreckage at the bottom of the incline.

"No, I can't feel my legs," Timothy remembers answering.

He recalled that he had been pulled through the shattered glass of the back windshield. Then blackness. Timothy Alexander, who ran so gracefully on a football field and whose smile could light up a room, now was paralyzed from the waist down. A future of catching passes in college and the NFL was gone. Victories for Timothy were going to be much more immediate. He would have to learn how to maneuver a wheelchair. Learn how to hold a pencil. Learn how to eat.

But first he would have to live ... and that was no certainty.

"The doctors promised his mother nothing," Van Phillips, the school principal, said.

When his vital signs didn't stabilize as hoped, his doctors administered a tracheotomy, slicing his windpipe to insert a tube to his lungs as a preventative measure in case his ability to breathe on his own became obstructed. At least once, doctors rushed a crash cart into his room and used defibrillators to shock his heart after his pulse flat-lined on the EKG.

"He was dying," Patricia said. "He was almost dead."

The pain was unbearable. Because of the tracheotomy, Timothy couldn't talk. He knew sign language, so when nurses asked him to describe his pain on a level of 1-to-10, with 10 being the worst, his answer would always be 10.

"I knew he was in such terrible pain because there were big tears rolling down his cheeks," Patricia remembered.

But he did stabilize, and by mid-December, he was moved to a rehabilitation center where he was to learn the realities of life without the use of his legs. At first, it didn't seem real to Timothy. "Three weeks and I'll be out of here," Timothy whispered his uncle, Wayne Woolf. But it would not be so simple. The reality? Doctors said Timothy would never walk again.

"They said I might never twist or turn again," Timothy recalled. And because of his brain injury, "they said I might not ever be able to read or write again."

"I did not value what the doctors said," Patricia recalled. "I know God is real and I know God works miracles. They always said never. Their word was never. But I know what God said, and when they told me never, I listened to them but I would always hear the voice of the Lord saying, 'It's in my hands.' I believed in my heart that Timothy would walk again."

As the depression hit him hard, he looked at Patricia. "Mom, if I'm going to be like this for the rest of my life," he said, "just tell them to pull the plug."

The words stung his mother.

"Timothy was thinking in his mind that his whole life had been taken away from him," Patricia Alexander recalled. "All of his dreams, all of his desires, everything that he wanted to do. He thought maybe that this was it. Deep down inside, he told me that he just wanted to die.

"Here he is, 17 years old, and everything is taken from him. Timothy did not want to live like that. I know he was in pain. I know he was in sorrow. I know he was heartbroken."

For Patricia, who had already lost her home and her middle son in 2006, the answers were in her faith. "With the help of the Lord," she said, "we could get through this."

Timothy developed terrible bed sores on his legs, back, buttocks and feet. But recover slowly he did, and by early 2007, when doctors sent him home, his uncle, Wayne, instead brought him right back and demanded he be re-admitted because Tim had a violent seizure, an uncontrollable fever and couldn't keep down any food. "He said, 'I'm sorry I am going to do this Tim, but I'm leaving you here because we can't help you at home," Timothy recalled. It was the right call. Timothy's sores had become severely infected and now bacteria raged through his body. More emergency surgery was needed.

But by spring 2007, Timothy actually was beginning to make remarkable physical progress. Therapy five days a week with Wayne taught him to function again in ways that allowed him to regain use of his arms, so that he could maneuver his wheelchair and provide basic care for himself. "He had to learn how to do everything again," Woolf said.

"It was just a miracle the way the Lord brought him back," Patricia said.

Early in 2007, Timothy began doing schoolwork from his bed at home. Teachers would visit him and go through assignments verbally. Amazingly, Timothy graduated with his high school class in May. Wayne helped him put on the cap and gown so Timothy could roll himself through the processional. His mother beamed with pride.

"I started crying before he ever even got up there because everybody was giving him a round of applause," Patricia said. "It was just such a blessing to see him graduate."

But beneath the ceremonial outfit, his feet were covered in soft slippers instead of shoes. The sores on his feet had become so enflamed that he couldn't wear regular footwear. And he was thin, so thin.

"I had gone from 195 pounds all the way down to 105 pounds," he said.

Soon it was back to the hospital. Timothy needed an additional major surgery, slicing away flesh from his buttocks, because of the infectious bed sores. This time, when they sent him home, doctors wanted him completely immobilized for six weeks. Even trips back to the doctor required an ambulance ride. With this setback, Timothy was in many ways at his darkest point.

He asked his mother to lean in close to him.

"He said, 'Mama, I would not wish this on my worst enemies,' and that stuck with me because most people want something bad to happen to their enemies.

"He asked me to forgive him of all the things he had done wrong, and for the past experiences he had in school. He was in a state where he was stuck in a bed and could not do anything. Everything that was done for Timothy, someone had to do it for him."

Laying there, Timothy was at his most vulnerable, helpless in his bed unable to move. Still, his mind had changed—for the better. "Mama, I don't want to die," he said. "I am so sorry."

Patricia leaned down to her son's ear, and spoke to him as only a mother could.

Photo courtesy of Patricia Alexander

After Timothy's accident, a sermon from Bishop Stephen A. Davis (left) led Timothy to turn away from his anger and seek a relationship with God.

"Timothy, you will not die," she said. "You are going to live and declare the works of the Lord. God kept you here for a reason. God is going to see you through this and God is going to use you in a mighty way that will lead people to Jesus."

In all, it took more than a year for Timothy to recover enough that he could begin to get his life back in order and come to grips with building a life in a wheelchair. By 2009, he enrolled in community college, where he wanted to pursue a degree in Criminal Justice. He got a car, learned how to drive it using special pedals, and was able to get from place to place. He was slowly gaining some independence. But to Timothy, it still seemed pointless and life was just about going through the motions. He didn't see a purpose or a future for himself. His mother, Patricia, grew upset at his lack of direction and habit of rolling in late from partying. She threatened to kick him out of the house and told him not to come home at all if he couldn't come in at a decent hour.

Then came an epiphany in 2010. He'd spent another night out at a club, but it was now Sunday morning. "I drove the car into the driveway after being out all night at the club and slept in the driveway," Timothy recalled. "I was still in the clothes I had worn out all night," Timothy said. "I remember waking up, and something telling me inside my head that I needed to go down to the church down the street."

Timothy rolled himself into the chapel. As he listened to the words from the back row, it seemed as if the pastor at New Birth Church in Center Point was speaking directly to Timothy. "Some of y'all are in here in the same clothes you had on at the club, smelling like drugs and alcohol," Bishop Stephen A. Davis told the congregation.

"And I'm looking around like, 'Is he talking to me?'" Timothy recalled. "The message was for everybody, but it just hit home."

Bishop Davis continued. "It's OK. God wanted you to be here because he is going to use you for something greater."

That day, Timothy asked God for forgiveness of his sins and "fell in love with the man who was preaching." He asked Bishop Davis to pray for him and to be his spiritual father. Bishop Davis told Timothy he would do so, but first he needed to come to church five

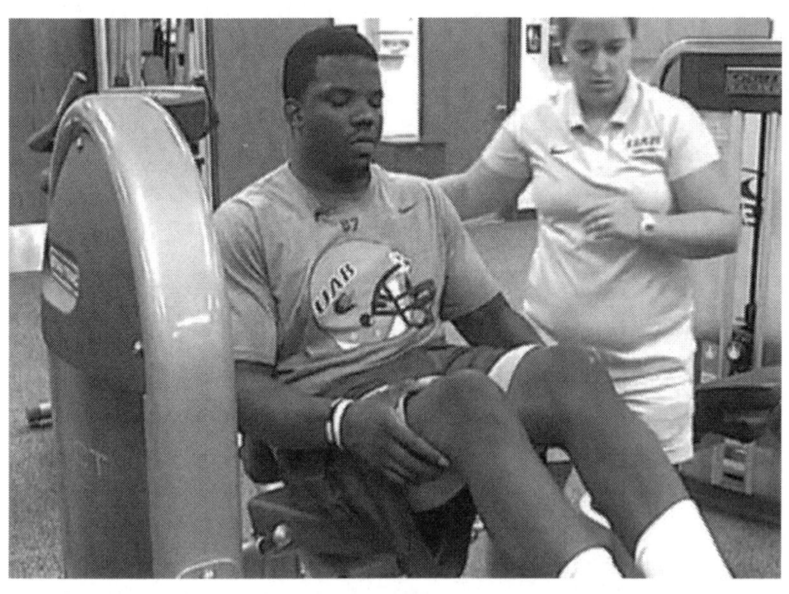

Timothy Alexander's long road to regaining use of his arms and other motor skills included grueling daily rehabilitation sessions.

times in a row, after which he would lay hands on him and pray for him and that God was going to use him to do something great in his life.

Timothy's outlook was soon going to change. Another pastor, Bishop Eddie Long, spoke at a revival. As Timothy prayed at the altar, Long told him that God's gift to him was that Timothy could inspire others by showing that God is faithful to those who are faithful to Him.

"From that point on, I just wanted to find God for myself," Timothy said. "It's not that I am a religious person as much as I am all about the relationship. I just threw myself into having a relationship with God."

It was during this period, while at the altar, that Timothy felt his first urge to stand. Friends held him by his arms as he strained to pull himself out of the wheelchair. To him, it felt as if he was standing with his feet on the floor. But that wasn't the case. Because his muscles were so atrophied, his legs remained curled as if they were still sitting in the chair.

He still had a long way to go when he transferred to the University of Alabama at Birmingham.

Then came an impossible dream.

7

Chapter

2nd Timothy

"Ma, I gotta go get some cleats! I'm going to play college football!" The vision was so vivid when Timothy awoke. He saw himself in his dream playing college football, running down the field, catching passes. He couldn't shake it.

"It was so very real to him," his mother, Patricia Alexander, said of the way Timothy described it.

By this time in 2011, Timothy had enrolled at the University of Alabama at Birmingham. And from this inspiration came a plan. Timothy stepped up the pace of his rehabilitation work. He began befriending Blazers student-athletes and became a fixture around UAB campus hangouts and athletic events. Then he wrote a letter to the Blazers' head football coach, Garrick McGee. He told the coach he'd been the No. 8- ranked player in the state of Alabama and asked to walk on. He explained that God had given him this vision and that he could bring success to the UAB program. The coach called Timothy in for a meeting in 2012.

He didn't really have a need for a tight end prospect in a wheelchair, but after the conversation, McGee decided to make room for Alexander on the team.

"I just fell in love with the person," McGee told CBSSports.com for a feature story produced midway through UAB's 2013 season, after Alexander had been part of the team for a year. "Then he started talking to me about, 'Man, the Lord is going to bless me. I'm going to be back on the field.' I started saying, 'You know, I believe that, too. I think you're right.'"

After that initial meeting with McGee, Timothy was sent to meet the team's athletic trainer, a former Blazer football player named Mike Jones. When he rolled into the training room, Timothy was met with a question: "You here to play football?" Jones asked him. "Yes, sir," was the reply.

From that point on, Timothy was treated as a

Photo courtesy of Steven Stiefel

Timothy grew up dreaming he might someday play college football at Legion Field in his hometown of Birmingham, Alabama. An actual dream after his accident set him on a course few people could have imagined.

player. He came to the training room daily. He did physical therapy in the morning. He went to class. He worked out in the afternoon. He went to study hall. Then at night, thanks to a friendship he had made with a member of the women's track team who also happened to be studying to become a physical therapist, he did more work to get stronger.

"It was in my heart that this was what I was going to school for, learning the body and the mechanics of the body, and I wanted to help him," Autumn Burnett said. "Going off of that, and that being my degree, I would go with him to his physical therapy appointments. I learned so much while I was there."

At night, she would go with Timothy to the UAB campus recreation center. There they would do more therapy, including crucial stretching exercises that helped Timothy gain flexibility and strength. They spent hours in the whirlpool. She gained knowledge; Timothy gained progress.

"He never gave up," she said. "The way that he works, his work ethic is incredible. I have never seen anybody who works like him, somebody who cannot stand up on his legs, with that mindset and drive. It is something not comparable to any athlete I have ever seen."

When the football team practiced, Alexander threw and caught passes on the sidelines. When his teammates did sprints, he did pushups. He studied the playbook, lifted weights, became what he called a "motivational player" who helped prepare his teammates mentally. He had a role, a locker, a jersey with the number 87, a bio on the team website—and, eventually, a scholarship.

"I became the first paraplegic football player to play football in the NCAA," he said.

"Tim was a player and that's how we looked at him," said Ty Long, the team's kicker from 2011-14.

But McGee abruptly quit as the Blazers' head coach at the end of the 2013 season, yet another dismal

Photo courtesy of Steven Stiefel

Timothy's influence on UAB's football program grew significantly when a new coach, Bill Clark (right), arrived to lead the Blazers in 2014. It didn't take him long to turn around the program, with Timothy playing a key role.

result on the field with a 2-10 record that included a season-ended 62-27 loss to rival Southern Miss in front of only 6,283 fans at 72,000-seat Legion Field in Birmingham. It was a dreary day that offered the absolute extreme of college football in football-crazy Alabama: While UAB was losing in front of thousands of empty seats to a Southern Miss team that had previously lost 23 consecutive games, Alabama and Auburn were playing one of college football's most-iconic games just two hours to the southeast. The 2013 Iron Bowl ended with a last-play, 100-yard kick return by Auburn on a missed field goal attempt—labeled forever as the Kick-Six—that dethroned Alabama as national champions and sent Auburn to the Rose Bowl to play for a national title of its own.

Perhaps sensing he was getting out of town before things turned worse for him the next season—or perhaps even sensing something even more nefarious — McGee made the peculiar career decision to resign as UAB's head coach in order to be the offensive coordinator at the University of Louisville.

McGee's departure left Timothy fearful for his future. What if a new coach didn't see a place on the team for a tight end who caught passes on the sidelines in a wheelchair?

On January 21, 2014, UAB introduced Bill Clark as its new head coach. He was fresh off a playoff appearance in his one season at his alma mater, Jacksonville State University in northeast Alabama, and had spent time as defensive coordinator at South Alabama after a distinguished career as a high school coach in Alabama. He was young —just 46 years old —energetic and he carried himself with the steely-eyed swagger of a man accustomed to rolling up his sleeves and winning.

Clark remembers his first meeting with the team. It was his chance to set a tone while also reading the body language of his new players, who had not experienced much success before his arrival.

"The first meeting for any program is a huge meeting," Clark said. "You've got one chance to make a first impression. That's a big meeting for me. One of the reasons it was so different (at UAB from other places he had coached) is that these guys were very, very downtrodden. One of the things I look for is eye contact. If a guy is making eye contact, he's hearing what I am saying, it's important to him. I can tell a level of confidence.

"This was not a good meeting from the standpoint of the look on the faces of the UAB players. They were down. They had lost their second coach in just a short time, how they lost their last coach was bad, and I think they were really doubting themselves."

One player caught Clark's eye: Timothy Alexander.

"I see a guy who is in the back of the room, and he's just all eyes on me. He's passionate-looking. He's energetic. He's glued into every word I am saying. That was Tim Alexander."

Clark didn't know the story. He didn't notice the wheelchair. He only saw a player who had the look of a potential leader, one whose presence struck him immediately. It was that same look Willie Miller had seen at Erwin High.

After the meeting, Alexander rolled up to his new head coach and began his story and asked if he could still be part of the team. The next day, Alexander went to meet his new coach to share the full story. Alexander was nervous that the new coach might not see a role for him, but those concerns quickly melted.

"There's no doubt we want you to be part of this team," Clark told him.

8

Chapter

Steps To The Top

Timothy Alexander was not a token member of the UAB football team. He would become its heart and soul.

"I put in the grind," Timothy said. "I would tell guys, you get down, you get tired, look over and watch me. I'm not going to quit. If I can do it, you can do it.

"I understand this—this race is not given to the swift or the strong but the one that can endure it to the end. I'm a young man of endurance. I have never seen the finish line in life because life is a constant race and you have to be willing to get better at it day in and day out, and that's just what I do."

His teammates respected that Timothy never asked for special consideration. When they scrimmaged, he did sit-ups and push-ups. He caught passes, he lifted weights. He pushed his body to the limit.

"He's a guy who is probably never going to get out on the field," receiver JJ Nelson said, "but it meant a lot to us that he came out every day, he worked out early in the morning, late in the afternoon. It motivated me and the other players to continue to get better."

Timothy was both a student of the game and a student of the game's psychology.

"Tim is always that guy to encourage you at times you would never know it was needed," UAB tight end Tristan Henderson said. "You would think that everything would be OK, and then here comes Tim talking to you, and you start recognizing things about yourself and about the way you approach everyday life. It inspires people because of the fact that he continues to push through anything and everything that falls in his way. It makes you want to be better."

*** *** ***

A bonding moment came on Valentine's Day in 2014.

Coach Bill Clark, completing his first month on the job, was looking for a rallying point to pull together a collection of individuals who had not experienced success. The idea that he and his new strength and conditioning coach, Zac Woodfin, discussed was to move a workout from campus over to historic Legion Field, where UAB played its home games.

As Woodfin remembered, the goal was not to break down the team, but to bring it together. For him, this was a labor of tough love. Woodfin was himself a former Blazer, starring at linebacker under Watson Brown. When he played his final game in 2004, he left for a brief NFL career as UAB's all-time leading tackler.

He had been working as a strength and conditioning coach with the Green Bay Packers when he got a call from his former coach at Prattville High. That coach, Bill Clark, was calling him home.

"People told me I was crazy to leave the Packers to come to UAB," Woodfin said, "but UAB was my alma mater and this was my program and Bill Clark was my coach."

Woodfin had watched the Blazers' struggles over the years after his final season captaining the defense, which had ended with the team's only bowl appearance. This was his opportunity to help fix it. So here he was, just a few days back at UAB and not even yet officially announced as part of the program, putting his new stamp on it. The instructions from Clark were simple.

"I wanted to take them over where we play and make that a place where they have paid a price," Clark recalled. "There is a symbolism to climbing that mountain. That's where we're going to look back as a team and remember what price we paid."

It was a cold day. The players were in sweatpants and sweatshirts, but soon those would be damp with sweat. To put it bluntly, the workout was brutal. It ended with players sprinting up Legion Field's bleachers, 75 steps or more each time they went to the top. Then back down. Then up again. Over and over.

Woodfin doesn't remember how many times, exactly, but it was a lot.

"Those stadium steps, they ain't no joke," Ty Long, the kicker, recalled. "They get steeper as you go up, so every rep, they get harder."

"I remember running, and not being able to breathe," said Henderson. "I was at the top. I was laying on the ground and I was breathing hard. I couldn't

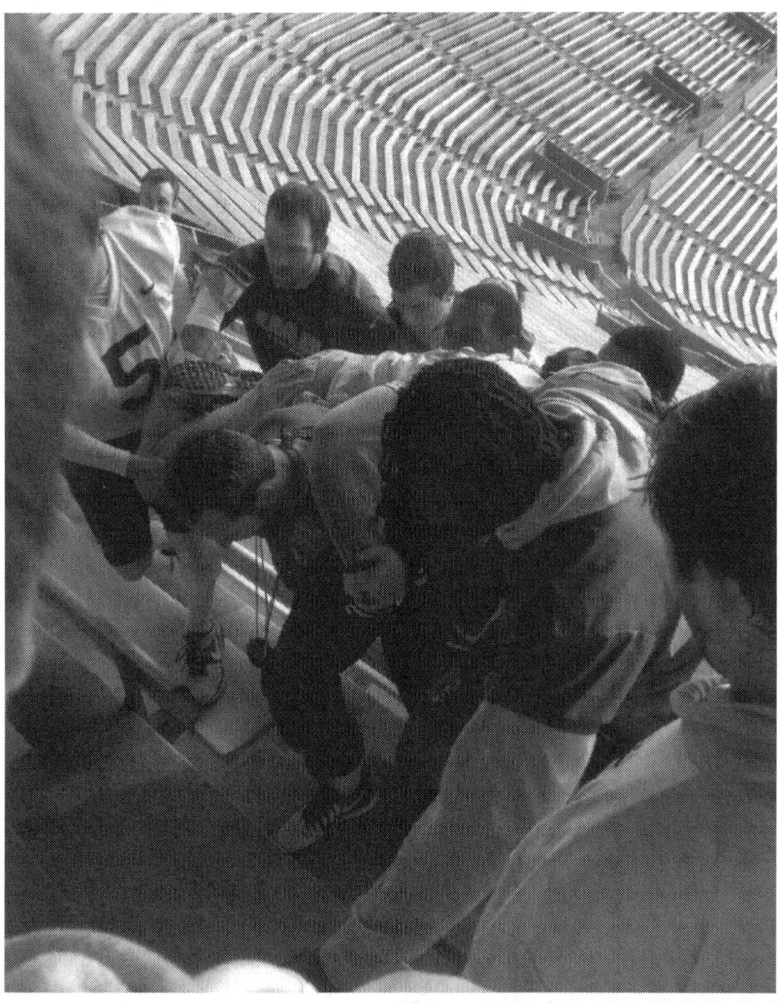

Photo courtesy of Jake Ganus/UAB Football

A powerful moment before the start of the 2014 season helped turn around the Blazers' fortunes when assistant coach Zac Woodfin and the rest of the team carried Timothy Alexander to the top of Legion Field.

even pick my legs up. It was bad. We were beat up pretty bad."

Jordan Howard, the star running back who now plays for the NFL's Chicago Bears, was among the team's strongest players and one of its hardest workers. Even he was feeling the burn.

"It was hard, especially hard on your legs, going down and up. It was a tough day to make it through. A few people started cramping up so bad they couldn't finish and guys were getting dizzy. It was very tough."

Nelson, one of the fastest players in college football in 2014, preferred running to other exercises the Blazers did in training. But even for him, this was no easy day. He tried to fight through it by being an example for his teammates. "At the end of the day, we didn't leave anybody behind. We all got through it."

And that meant *everybody*.

Clark called for everyone to run to the top, including all the injured players. Woodfin noticed Alexander in his wheelchair at the bottom the stadium steps. Timothy had been there, doing push-ups against the chain-link fence, while his teammates ran. Woodfin saw the pained look in Alexander's eyes. He knew what he had to do.

"I didn't even have time to think about it, really," Woodfin said. "I ran over and asked him if he wanted to go to the top."

Of course, Timothy said yes.

And so they did.

*** *** ***

Going to the top of the stadium meant Woodfin would lift Alexander onto his back and walk.

"I took him over my shoulders like a fireman's carry," Woodfin said.

One step. Two. Three. And on and on. Up and up.

"I quickly realized, 'I am in trouble here,' " Woodfin said. "Tim Alexander is a big man. He's 6-foot-5, 260 pounds. And he can't help me, so I've got to carry his full weight."

Howard saw what was happening and was astonished. "I couldn't believe he was doing it," Howard said. "It took a lot of strength to do that. You don't realize it when Tim is in his wheelchair, but if you ever see him standing up out of his chair with someone holding him, he is a *huge* guy."

To cap a team-changing workout at Legion Field, UAB strength and conditioning coach Zac Woodfin carries Timothy Alexander on his shoulders to the top of the stadium.

Timothy, of course, couldn't really help Woodfin other than to hold on with his arms. At one point, Timothy's body shifted and his head tilted inches away from the cement steps.

"I told him, 'Don't you drop me,' Timothy recalled with a smile.

Woodfin's arms and legs burned as if doused with gasoline and set afire. His body began to shake with each step. His lungs begged for air. They weren't even halfway yet.

"Tim, start praying," Woodfin told him.

"Jesus, Jesus, Jesus," Tim repeated over and over as they continued on.

Other players, scattered throughout the stadium as they ran, began to notice what was happening.

"I don't know who said it, but this was said verbatim: 'Holy shit, Coach Woodfin is carrying Tim up Legion.'" Henderson said. "Those are the words I heard. I did my damnedest to move. I rolled over and looked down, and you could see it coming, step by step, step by step. They get halfway, and one of the other coaches runs down and grabs Tim's legs, and they keep coming, step by step."

Said Long: "When Woodfin did that, it showed you what kind of guy Zac is and the kind of staff Bill Clark had put together."

Other coaches and players joined in, helping Woodfin and Alexander through the agony. One step at a time. Together. When one man faltered, another stepped in.

All the way to the top.

Now surrounded by players, and with whoops and hollers urging them on, they took the final step. Woodfin collapsed.

"I've never been so tired in my life," he said. "I must have laid there like ten minutes."

As the coach caught his breath, Timothy reminded him of something: "How are we going to get back down?"

That brought a big laugh followed by a sigh of relief as players brought Timothy's wheelchair to the top of the stadium and then discovered an elevator from the concourse to the ground.

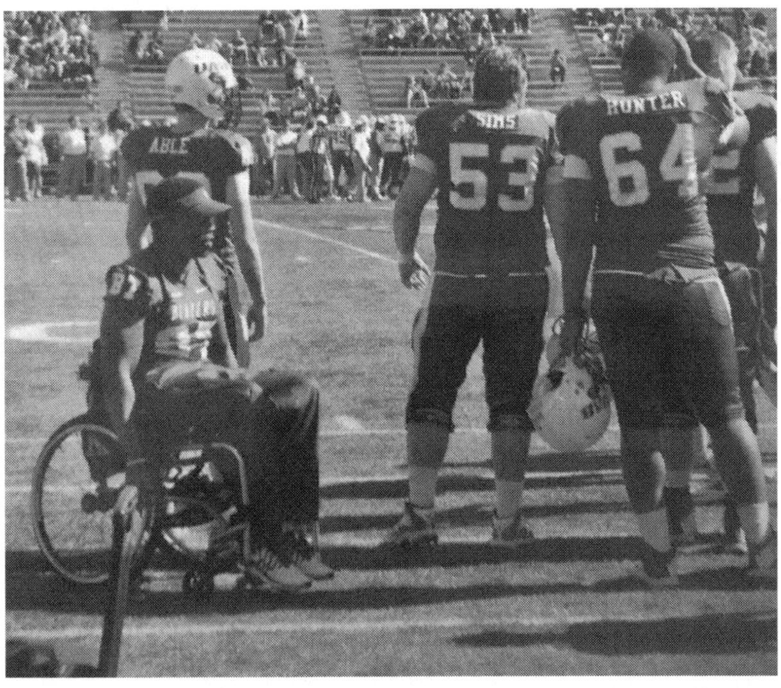

Photo courtesy of Patricia Alexander

Timothy Alexander was not a token part of the UAB football team in 2013 and 2014. He was believed to be the first paraplegic athlete to earn an NCAA Division I football scholarship.

Watching it all unfold, Clark knew he was witnessing the turning point for the Blazers. Everyone did.

"We're gonna be good!" Henderson remembers someone yelling.

"We were already a close team, but that cemented it," Howard said.

"Of all the moments of 29 years, and being a coach's son, that was probably one of the most powerful moments I have ever been a part of," Clark said. "Totally spontaneous. ... We said, 'Everybody to the top. We're all going to up together.' Tim said, 'That means me, too.' Zac jumped in there, and he's in really good shape — he's not a player but he's still in really good shape — and he takes Tim on his back. He gets a few steps up, I mean, maybe five or 10 steps up is all, and I'm thinking he's not going to be able to make it. And then a few come and help and then we've got the whole team. Zac's legs are shaking, and I'm watching this team come together.

"Everybody out there was crying. It was that strong of a moment. I called my wife when it was over and told her I had just witnessed one of the greatest things I had ever seen. I get choked up thinking about it. That was a moment of change. You couldn't have scripted it. They needed it. It was real. It was organic. It was symbolic. For me, getting to watch it all, it changed *me*."

Henderson, the senior tight end who had previously served in military before enrolling at UAB, saw it even more succinctly.

"That was the moment I knew we were about to be good," Henderson recalled. "Ever since Coach Clark got there in the spring, there was this coffin and in that coffin was all the stuff from the past: the cliques, the losses, people not giving effort, people not caring about each other. All that stuff is in the coffin and every single day we are putting a nail in it.

All of the demons that the program had, all of the craziness, everything was being put in that coffin and in that moment it was the final nail to say it's all behind us, let's move forward."

9

Chapter

Political Football

UAB players knew things were going to be different in 2014. Fans quickly figured it out. In Bill Clark's first game, the new-look Blazers in no way resembled their predecessors that had not produced a winning season since 2004. Wearing flashy modern uniforms and shiny gold helmets emblazoned with a sleek dragon's head, the Blazers smoked rival Troy University 48-10 in front of 27,133 at Legion Field.

A week later in Starkville, Miss., there came even a stronger indication that Clark was on his way to turning the Blazers around. UAB held a second-quarter lead and would go on to lose by only 13 points, 47-34, to a Mississippi State team led by future Dallas Cowboys quarterback Dak Prescott that would eventually spend time ranked No. 1 in the country.

"That first game against Troy, we came out and beat them badly," said Jordan Howard, who in 2014 would set a school record for rushing yards in a season. "Troy had beaten us the year before, but they didn't even have a chance in that game. Then we came out and played Mississippi State toe-to-toe. That's when we knew we could have a pretty good year."

Blazers fans, downtrodden for so long, could see signs of the turnaround not just in game results but in the language of the head coach and in the way the team carried itself. Bill Clark was a winner. The Blazers were going to be winners, too ... quicker than anyone imagined.

Photo courtesy of Shannon Brasher Ritch
As the team's "motivational player," Timothy Alexander had a sideline view of the Blazers' turnaround season under first-year coach Bill Clark in 2014.

"There was a feeling that we finally had the right coach," said Paul Ensign, a longtime UAB fan and owner of the fan website BlazerTalk.com. "For the longest time there had been a feeling among fans that we were like Charlie Brown trying to kick the football, and just when we were going to kick it, Lucy would yank it away. This time it felt different. It felt real."

But Lucy planned to take her football and go home.

Wins over Alabama A&M, Western Kentucky and North Texas gave UAB a 4-2 record at the season's halfway point. But even before Clark had played his first month of games, trouble was on the horizon. Unknown to anyone except a few high-level administrators, plans were already being explored by the administration to shut down the UAB football program. The conspiracy theories would grow loud during the final month of the 2014 season.

To understand how UAB football came to be on the chopping block just as it appeared a talented young coach would turn it into a winner, one must understand the politics of the state of Alabama and the history between the upstart campus in Birmingham and its main campus in Tuscaloosa, founded in 1831 and home of the mighty Crimson Tide.

Academically, there had come to be intense competition between the three campuses of the UA System, which included the main campus in Tuscaloosa and branches in Huntsville and Birmingham, the state's largest city. Originally founded as an extension center in 1936, the Birmingham campus was granted autonomy with its own president under the direction of the UA System in 1969 and quickly established itself as one of the top medical schools and research centers in the United States. By 1992, UAB had been ranked the No. 1 "Up and Coming University" in the prestigious annual rankings by *U.S. News & World Report*.

"The flagship institution doesn't really want the other ones to exist," said Dr. John Knox, who was one of the first students recruited to the UAB Honors Program, became UAB's first national finalist to become a Rhodes Scholar and now is a faculty member at the University of Georgia. The Tuscaloosa campus, he said, viewed the city campuses more as colonies to be mined rather than competitors for attention.

"This has always been the theme—not just athletics," Knox said. "For decades and decades, everything has been a fight. This is the mindset, unfortunately."

The growth of the extension centers threatened to upset the political balance of power in the state, which had been controlled for decades by Tuscaloosa, home of the law school. With the Birmingham campus beginning to gain political clout, securing a larger slice of state funding and clamoring for representation on the powerful Board of Trustees, the tensions grew. Only in Alabama would one run for governor, as Lt. Gov. Bill Baxley did, with advertisements that proclaimed "Bill Baxley will not let The University become U.A.T." The advertisements were paid for by a group chaired by Paul Bryant Jr., son of the legendary Crimson Tide football coach, Paul "Bear" Bryant.

"How dare the little sister stand up to the big sister?" said Dr. Kristie Rankin, an avid UAB supporter and alumnus who also holds degrees from the University of Alabama. "There are always politics involved in everything here. We live in a state where if you move from another state to Alabama, the two questions you are going to be asked are: 1) Are you Baptist or Catholic; and 2) Who you for? And by that, they mean Alabama or Auburn.

"If you look historically, people made fun of us for bringing up The Machine, but anyone from Alabama knows about The Machine (a fraternity-based secret political society at UA). It's a real thing. It runs politics in the state of Alabama, and you know who came out of the University of Alabama and who is tied to what political group at the University of Alabama, and who went on to become senators, governors and representatives. They are all connected in one way or another, and it's all politically linked to the University of Alabama.

"It's no surprise that football became part of politics."

The politics predated the university system to some degree. Tuscaloosa represented Old South aristocracy, the land-owning "Big Mules" as they were called, who pulled the levers of power in the state. Birmingham? It was a steel city founded by carpet-bagging northerners during the post-Civil War Reconstruction in 1871 to create the "Pittsburgh of the South." It was a diverse city that would come to be the center of the Civil Rights movement in the 1960s while the Tuscaloosa campus attempted to fight integration of the university with Gov. George Wallace's famous stand in the schoolhouse door. While Birmingham might be the economic engine of the state, it was often met with suspicion and derision from other regions of Alabama. This put UAB very much into the spotlight as the steel industry gave way to a medical-based economy.

"The UAB miracle," Knox calls it. "Dream for the stars and will it into being," despite a governance structure that seemed to expect a less-comprehensive vision for the university mission.

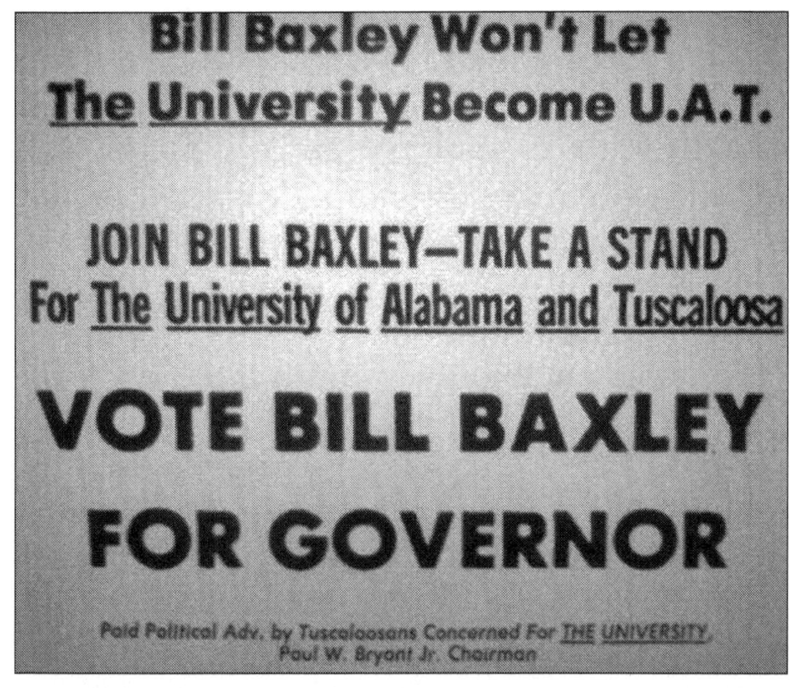

The political rivalry runs deep in the relationship between the Tuscaloosa and Birmingham campuses of the UA System. With Paul Bryant Jr., son of the legendary Crimson Tide football coach, advising his campaign, Bill Baxley even ran for governor promising to protect the main campus in Tuscaloosa.

Sports, in no small way, became a symbol of it all.

From the start, UAB dreamed big in sports. Gene Bartow, successor to legendary basketball coach John Wooden at UCLA, was hired as the school's basketball coach and athletic director in 1977, and in only its third season of NCAA competition, the upstart Blazers reached the Sweet Sixteen of the NCAA Tournament. They reached the Elite Eight a year later, beating powerhouse programs such as Indiana, Kentucky and a Virginia team led by Ralph Sampson, the national Player of the Year, during those memorable back-to-back seasons.

But football was never supposed to be part of the plan at UAB, where the arrival of Gene Bartow as basketball coach was met with then-university president S. Richardson Hill holding up a bumper sticker that read, "UAB 1, UCLA 0," and where years later the Tuscaloosa News would proclaim in an editorial that "only a genie could bring football to UAB."

The clear message was that the Birmingham campus dare not compete with the "main campus" in Tuscaloosa, where Coach Paul "Bear" Bryant's Crimson Tide ruled college football. When Bartow arrived in Birmingham in 1977, Bryant was on his way to winning his fifth and sixth national championships with the mighty Tide, and Birmingham was his town. Legion Field, the storied "Football Capital of the South," hosted Alabama's big games against Tennessee and the Iron Bowl against Auburn, as well as Alabama's big non-Southeastern Conference games against national powers such as Nebraska, Southern Cal and Notre Dame.

A decade after integration in the SEC, Birmingham was Bryant's prime recruiting hotbed for talent. So, of course, Bryant was none too keen on the idea of a new football program rising up in his backyard, playing in *his* stadium. Especially one from the University of Alabama System.

He also didn't have to look far to see validation of that idea, because at the time UAB was launching athletics, the upstart University of Houston was having the audacity to start beating Texas, win the Southwest Conference and play in the Cotton Bowl. No, whatever politics might be at play, Bryant's opposition had roots in competition.

Bartow enjoyed a run of basketball success in the 1980s, with seven consecutive berths in the NCAA Tournament and two trips to the Sweet 16. But he also understood the changing college athletics landscape, driven by television, and he believed UAB ultimately would need big-time football to thrive in an era of conference realignment in the decades to come. His goal was to align UAB with what he saw as its peer institutions, urban universities such as Houston, Louisville, South Florida in Tampa, Cincinnati and Memphis State, which he had led to the 1973 NCAA Tournament championship game.

The topic of UAB football made for pointed conversation on talk radio, especially as a basketball feud emerged between Bartow and Alabama coach Wimp Sanderson. Their recruiting battles further fueled a rivalry that didn't actually exist on the court — Alabama refused to play UAB in basketball and most sports.

When Bartow began pushing for a football team in the mid-1980s, it met unofficial resistance from the board of trustees.

"It came up (informally) about two years ago and a pretty clear negative view was taken at that time," then-UA System Chancellor Thomas Bartlett told the Birmingham Post-Herald in 1986. "Nothing has come along and changed that."

Then-trustee Cleo Thomas was more more emphatic, telling the Post-Herald at that time: "I just hope we don't forget what the chief mission of UAB is, and that it's the medical school. If this came up to the board, it would be voted down. But I can't see it coming up. It is in the character of those at UAB to want to climb the mountain. But I think the consensus would be to put their energy elsewhere. Some might say they have a football team — the one in Tuscaloosa."

When asked about the possibility of football at UAB in 1989, then-Alabama coach Bill Curry dismissed the idea entirely: "Not only would we not play them, we don't understand why they are talking about bringing another football team into the University of Alabama system," Curry said. "I'm the only (football) coach in the University of Alabama system. We don't need another football team at one of our other campuses."

But Bartow persisted. In 1989, UAB launched a club football team, and then-UAB president Charles

"Scotty" McCallum launched an NCAA non-scholarship Division III team in 1991 with former Auburn assistant coach Dr. Jim Hilyer as head coach, leading a staff of former college and pro stars with Birmingham or Alabama ties.

"Dr. McCallum brought up football to the board, and the board said they would be against it," recalled Gary Sanders, the radio voice of UAB athletics from 1979 to 2006. "He said, 'That's a presidential decision, and I've made the decision we're going to have it.'"

Whether the board liked it or not, football was now reality at UAB, and with Bartow pressing behind the scenes, it was only a matter of time before the Blazers moved up. When an NCAA rule was passed requiring all Division I athletic programs who played football to also play that sport at the Division I level, there was a window to accelerate plans. UAB moved to scholarship FCS (Division I-AA) in 1993 and in 1994 announced the program would move to FBS (Division I-A) in 1996. Soon after, the first opponent was announced: Auburn, at Jordan-Hare Stadium.

The early years of UAB football were surprisingly good. Hilyer's coaching staff included a handful of former pro players, such as former NFL rookie of the year Dieter Brock and former Buffalo Bills All-Pro running back Joe Cribbs. The Blazers posted a 27-12 record in the first four seasons and three players recruited by Hilyer's staff would go on to play in the NFL.

"Every time we went on the field, we realized that if we won, we could build a program," said Josh

Evans, who starred for the Blazers on their first four teams before going on to start at defensive tackle for the Houston Oilers/Tennessee Titans and New York Jets in the NFL. "Guys realized that you are not just playing for yourself, for your team, but you are playing for the future."

After 1994, Bartow brought in former Vanderbilt head coach Watson Brown to lead the program into the big time. In 1995, his first season, the Blazers earned their first victory over a Division I-A team when they won at North Texas. And in that 1996 opener at Auburn, the Blazers played surprisingly tough against the Tigers, trailing only 9-0 at halftime before losing 29-0. Rarely had the Plains been so quiet against an opponent some had predicted Auburn might beat by 100 points.

"It was an auspicious start," said Sanders, who before becoming the UAB radio announcer had spent several years as the radio voice for Auburn sports.

"We all had something to prove," said UAB quarterback/receiver Kevin Drake, who was the first offensive player signed to a football scholarship by UAB and would go on to play in the NFL with the Dallas Cowboys and Arizona Cardinals. "We all played with a chip on our shoulder because we all felt we were overlooked and for many of us, like me, UAB was our only opportunity to prove we could play at that level."

Slowly and steadily, Brown was building up a competitive team while transitioning into membership in Conference USA. The upstart program would soon come of age on a muggy night in Death Valley.

10

Chapter

Board Games

On Sept. 23, 2000, UAB went into Baton Rouge, La., and upset the mighty LSU Tigers 13-10 in Death Valley on a last-second field goal. Imagine that. A school that didn't even own a football in 1990 had—in less than 10 years—joined college football's highest classification and knocked off one of its legendary coaches—Nick Saban—in one of the game's most hallowed venues. On LSU's homecoming, no less.

Probably even more importantly than the games themselves, the UA System Board of Trustees gained a famous new member that fall: Paul Bryant Jr., son of the legendary Alabama coach. A few months later, program founder Gene Bartow retired as UAB's athletics director. That same year, the Board of Trustees created a new athletics committee to oversee the athletic departments of all three campuses in Tuscaloosa, Birmingham and Huntsville. It was a self-perpetuating board, essentially reporting to no one else, in which virtually all of the members were graduates of the Tuscaloosa campus.

Coincidences?

"It was essentially the only situation in the NCAA where you had some of the largest boosters of one Division I university overseeing and controlling the direction of another Division I university's athletics department," said Jack Williams, a state representative from Vestavia Hills, a suburb of Birmingham.

With one of the nation's top-ranked defenses, the UAB football program posted its first FBS winning record in 2000 with a 7-4 mark. It followed up with a 6-5 mark in 2001. In both cases, it was left out of a bowl game, but the progress seemed solid. Attendance was meager by the standards of the state's SEC behemoths, but it was in line with UAB's peer institutions, and

Photo courtesy of UAB Archives

UAB president S. Richardson Hill (left) hired coach Gene Bartow away from UCLA to start a big-time basketball program in Birmingham. As athletics director, Bartow came to believe UAB also needed a big-time football program to compete in a changing college sports landscape. Bartow succeeded in both efforts, but made powerful enemies along the way.

Blazer fans were giddy. With several players headed to the NFL and a great recruiting class on the way, fans expected UAB to become a contender for the Conference USA championship.

Then on the day before the 2002 NFL Draft, a draft in which two Blazer defensive linemen were projected to be selected in the first round, the UA Board of Trustees issued an edict: Make money within two years or the program would be shut down.

Black Friday, UAB fans called it.

"The Board of Trustees basically knee-capped us," said Paul Ensign, owner of the fan website BlazerTalk.com. "What kind of board would do that to their team? If you are concerned about money, shouldn't you help raise money?"

To solve the immediate needs, Watson Brown became athletic director as well as head coach. An aggressive fund-raising campaign began, although money couldn't specifically be donated for football in the way that Alabama boosters could donate to UA's new Crimson Tide Foundation. UAB began more aggressively scheduling "money games" on the road against powerful programs that added to the bank account but also added to the loss column. By the summer of 2003, the board backed off that make-money-or-else edict, but to a large degree, the damage had already been done, even if it didn't show up on the field immediately.

The 2004 Blazers, led by All-American wide receiver Roddy White, won seven games and earned the program's first bowl appearance, a loss to Hawaii in the

Hawaii Bowl. Along the way they beat established programs such as Baylor, Cincinnati, TCU and Mississippi State and were briefly ranked in the Bowl Championship Series standings at No. 24.

What should have been a season that established UAB as a legitimate college football program instead became its high-water mark. Recruiting had been crippled. Brown began to show the effects of running the entire athletic department in addition to the football team, and the bottom fell out. At the end of a dismal 2006 season in which a senior-laden Blazers team won only three games, Brown left to become head coach at Tennessee Tech in his hometown of Cookeville, Tenn.

From there, a series of events unfolded that most UAB fans described as Board of Trustees shenanigans.

* A plan to promote UAB offensive coordinator Pat Sullivan, the former Heisman Trophy winner at Auburn, to head coach was shot down. Sullivan left to become head coach at crosstown FCS school Samford University.

* UAB administrators thought they had a deal to hire LSU offensive coordinator Jimbo Fisher as coach, with boosters paying a large chunk of the salary. That deal was shot down, too, also amid rumors that the board had interfered in hopes that Fisher might be available to join the staff of new Alabama coach Nick Saban. Fisher eventually landed at Florida State, where he won the national championship in 2013. He left for Texas A&M in the fall of 2017 as the highest-paid coach in college football with his 10-year, $75-million contract.

* Into the void came former Alabama offensive lineman Neil Callaway, the offensive coordinator at Georgia. Callaway had played for Bear Bryant at Alabama. He had an SEC pedigree and a good reputation for developing offensive linemen, but the hiring was met with mixed reactions by fans who questioned why UAB would hire a coach who hadn't been in demand elsewhere and had recently been stripped of play-calling duties in his previous role.

* With Callaway struggling on the field and attendance lagging at aging Legion Field, UAB president Carol Garrison developed a plan for a $75 million, 30,000-seat on-campus stadium. On the day it was expected to be approved in November 2011, the Board of Trustees instead pulled the project off the agenda, calling it "the wrong project at the wrong time."

"A majority of the Board believes that an on-campus football stadium is not in the best interest of UAB, the University System or the State," it said. "It is the Board's duty to be responsible stewards of the limited resources available for higher education. In these difficult economic times of rising tuition and decreasing state funds, we cannot justify the expenditure of $75 million in borrowed money for an athletic stadium which would only be used a few days each year. The UAB football program has not generated sufficient student, fan or financial support to assure the viability of this project."

By then, Paul Bryant Jr. had been promoted to president pro tempore of the Board of Trustees, and wielded substantial power.

In retrospect, perhaps that statement should have been a warning sign. Callaway was fired after five seasons and an 18-42 record. UAB quickly moved to hire Arkansas assistant coach Garrick McGee in hopes that the Broyles Award winner as the nation's top assistant coach, as well as Alabama's first African-American head coach at an FBS school, could inject some life into the

What's Ablaze

UAB shocks SEC

Rhett Gallego kicks game winning field goal to upset LSU 13-10

Into the Streets

BSAC Stepshow

Who's Who

Photo courtesy Tim Stephens/UAB Kaleidoscope

UAB President Charles "Scotty" McCallum launched football at UAB against the board of trustees' wishes in 1991. From that first NCAA Division III game against Millsaps College on Sept. 7, 1991 (top), UAB fans dreamed of someday competing in college football's highest division. It would be a rapid rise for the Blazers, who made headlines across the nation (bottom) when they shocked LSU 13-10 in Tiger Stadium in 2000.

program.

McGee instead went 5-19 in two seasons (2012 and 2013) before abruptly departing to join Bobby Petrino's staff at Louisville. Fundraising and attendance were at all-time lows. University subsidies of athletics had grown by millions at a time when the escalating arms race among conferences had skyrocketed. UAB had some of the worst facilities in FBS, played in one of the worst stadiums and was coming off a blowout loss to a team that had previously lost 23 consecutive games.

Some people might see that lack of success as a reflection of community interest in the product, that UAB football had poor results on and off the field because it had been an ill-conceived idea from the start. Others saw the outcome as the self-fulfilling prophecy of inadequate administrative commitment, and whether that was ambivalent neglect or hostile subterfuge was a matter of interpretation. Had the board truly tacked UAB football to the wall like a fly to sadistically watch it squirm for a decade? Well, no one from the board was going to acknowledge such, but, as SEC Network analyst Paul Finebaum noted on ESPN, "Whether that was true or not, perception does matter."

And that perception was backed up by, at least on the surface, a track record.

"When Jimbo Fisher wanted to come to UAB, and that looked like it was going to be a done deal, they had the plane all set to go get him, and the board scuttled it," CBS Sports' Jon Solomon said. "When you end up hiring Neil Callaway instead of Jimbo Fisher, that's pretty telling. Nick Saban was just starting at Alabama and they needed to get Nick an offensive coordinator; the powers that be may have wanted (Fisher) at Alabama as an offensive coordinator instead of at UAB as a head coach. He probably wouldn't have stayed at UAB very long, but it is pretty hard to say you are going to hire Neil Callaway over Jimbo Fisher."

Now Callaway was gone. McGee was gone. And program founder Gene Bartow was gone, too. Bartow, who won more than 600 games as a college basketball coach and had built UAB athletics from start-up to Conference USA membership before retiring, passed away after a two-year battle with stomach cancer in January 2012. Those close to Bartow feared it would be only a matter of time until old enemies came to bury his legacy: Blazer football.

"Gene Bartow, out of his mouth, told me on many, many occasions that the aim of the board of trustees was to kill UAB football in the last 8-10 years," UAB booster Jimmy Filler told CBSSports.com in November 2014. "They're going to get the recommendation (from UAB President Ray Watts), and they'll accept what he brings to them."

This was the mess of a program Bill Clark walked into in January 2014.

11

Chapter

Blazer Betrayal

Timothy Alexander didn't know any of the conspiracy theories when he joined the UAB football program in 2013. And all he knew in 2014 was that UAB had a great new coach who had immediately infused the program with a winning attitude. As UAB athletic director Brian Mackin had said in a meeting of the selection committee, "If I can get Bill Clark, I like my chances."

Timothy certainly had every reason to believe that, too.

But there were signs that something was amiss. For starters, Clark had only been signed to a three-year contract rather than the standard five-year deal given to most coaches. And then a few former players had gotten wind that the university had stopped scheduling non-conference football games into the future. A $1-million donation to refurbish the turf at a practice field was rejected. Word leaked that the school had done only a one-year lease agreement with the city for use of Legion Field for home games. Further, a study had been commissioned by the administration to assess athletic department needs. Fears began to emerge that this study was not a "wish list," but rather was being used to justify a decision to end the football program.

In November, with UAB pushing toward bowl eligibility, prominent UAB boosters began pushing for answers. But they were not getting any beyond vague statements from the university that no decision had been made as the university pursued its "strategic review."

For some, that was an answer.

"If you can't answer your former players, letterman, alumni and community leaders — and people

Photo courtesy of City of Birmingham

With his teammates behind him, Timothy Alexander implores the Birmingham City Council to stand behind the Blazers amid rumors the UAB football program could be shut down at the end of the 2014 season. It would be the first of dozens of speeches Timothy would give in his efforts to save the team.

who are wanting to bring dollars and support - to me I knew something was really, really wrong," said Justin Craft, a former UAB player from 1994-96. Now the senior vice president at one of Birmingham's leading financial services firms, Craft in early November sounded the alarm to the UAB fan base and tried to work with administrators to kick-start efforts to raise money. "It was troubling."

Timothy Alexander also did his part to raise awareness. He and dozens of members of the team attended a meeting of the Birmingham City Council on November 18, 2014, days before UAB's final home game. Timothy spoke for five minutes, recounting how he, in many ways, was the epitome of the UAB football story. Given no chance, he had achieved many of his life dreams through the opportunities created by UAB football and support from his teammates. He asked the council to support keeping the football program. He shared the story of his coaches and teammates who had carried him to the top of Legion Field. "If you meet us halfway, we can continue to make it to the top," Timothy implored the council.

As he closed, teammates helped Timothy out of his wheelchair. With his arms draped around two of his UAB football brothers, Timothy faced the council as he stood on legs that could not move. "They told me I would never be able to do this," he said. There were audible gasps from the room, then applause, then chants of "U-A-B!" as Timothy made his final plea: "I'm asking you to stand up for UAB football with me today."

If the team was distracted by rumors, it didn't show. An offense led by future Chicago Bears running back Jordan Howard and future Arizona Cardinals receiver J.J. Nelson pushed the Blazers closer to bowl eligibility and started to attract more fans to Legion Field. By the time undefeated and 18th-ranked Marshall arrived at Legion Field for a November 22 game, more than 28,000 UAB fans gathered for what was essentially the Blazers' last stand. Marshall won 23-18 that day, scoring the go-ahead touchdown on a fumble recovery and then stopping Howard on fourth-down-and-one in the shadow of the UAB goal line in the closing minutes, but a statement had been made. The Blazers could compete with the best in Conference USA and had just posted the second-largest attendance average increase in FBS in 2014.

One game remained, at rival Southern Miss. Win and the Blazers would be bowl eligible for the first time since 2004.

"We went into that game thinking we could save the program," Timothy said. "We were fighting for our lives."

Craft was on the sidelines during the game and in the locker room after the Blazers blasted Southern Miss 45-24. "I don't know that I have ever seen a team come together like that team did that day. They played their hearts out. They really felt like, 'We're playing this game for the future of this program, and we've not only got to win, we've got to make a statement.' At the end of the game, they felt like they had done enough. I have been in a lot of locker rooms, but I have never seen a celebration that was so sincere, so full of emotion."

Craft held out hope as the Blazers piled up the points that day. "I never accepted it. For some strange reason, I kept thinking we would change their mind. We'll let them know that this matters and this can benefit the university and I hope the powers that be, whoever is making these decisions, would listen."

Truth be told, the decision had been prepared in large part before the Blazers had even played their first game of the season, never mind their last. The study conducted by longtime athletics administrator and consultant Bill Carr, which came to be derisively known as the Carr Report, concluded that UAB football wasn't economically viable and that as much as $49 million would need to be invested over five years to even have a chance to be competitive. University documents leaked after the decision showed talking points had been prepared months in advance, all the way down to conversations with players who would be cast out of the program. A public relations firm had been contracted to assist with messaging. One version of the documents actually called for the announcement to be made in mid-September, during a UAB open date, but noted the possibility for a player boycott was strong and that it would be advisable to wait until the end of the season. December 1 or December 2 were noted in those documents as the target dates for an announcement.

"They used the study as a justification, but I can get you a study that will say almost anything you want it to say," said Gary Sanders, the longtime radio announcer and confidante of program founder Gene Bartow. "You tell the guy beforehand what you want the survey to come back with, and that's what it will come back with."

Said investigative reporter Jon Solomon, who wrote extensively about the decision for CBSSports.com: "Who knows what Bill Carr's intentions were, but I think UAB wanted a certain outcome when they went into that process. We later found out, in documents released by Jack Williams, showing just how far back they were thinking about this and looking into it.

"They kept saying in November, 'no decision has been made,' when in fact there were documents showing that in September, the decision HAD been made that it would be the last year and there was a big-time crisis PR firm from New York that had been hired to handle the situation. They had talking points in September."

It all led to that horrible afternoon of December 2, when Dr. Ray Watts walked into an old building and pulled the life support.

Watts was never supposed to deliver that message. The script called for the athletic director, Brian Mackin, to do it. But Mackin quit before the meeting, leaving the university president to do the dirty work of informing the team, using the phrases that had been compiled months earlier.

That was victory number one in a coming resistance.

"He delivered the news that grandma was going to die, and there's nothing you or I can do about it," said Chuck Tuggle, a UAB alumnus who as a student had been one of the founding members of the club football program in 1989. "It's over, just say our peace and go on with it. The manner in which he delivered it was about as cold and callous at it could be."

The video of that delivery gave those who would fight the decision a visible villain to target. But for some diehard UAB supporters, the university president was merely a messenger, and whether he was part of the plot or merely carrying out an order from above him didn't matter. No statements or studies would ever change their position that killing the programs had been a dirty deed.

"It was a betrayal," said Birmingham media consultant Ralph Harbison, a former Mr. UAB winner, member of the inaugural UAB marching band in 1994 and former legislator in the UAB student government association. "It was a malicious act. It was done specifically to hurt people, and that makes it evil."

Publicly, the 17 members of the UA System Board of Trustees tried to stay out of the fray. Many phone calls from local and national media members weren't returned. Calls that were answered or returned generally were met with "no comment" or vague responses. Bryant, famously reclusive with media even long before he joined the board in 2000, waved off reporters with a "no" when they attempted to ask him about UAB football at a Crimson Tide baseball game.

If UAB football was born of a presidential decision by Dr. Charles "Scotty" McCallum in 1991, it died via presidential decision of Dr. Ray Watts in 2014.

Even the state's governor, who serves as president ex officio of the UA System board, stayed out of the controversy.

"I found out about it when y'all found out about it," Gov. Robert Bentley told reporters. "I'm not going to talk about UAB football, so that's all the questions I'm going to answer on that."

The silence didn't stop Bentley, who later would be forced out of office after a sex scandal, from cracking a joke about it. Speaking at a Nurses Day ceremony at the state capitol in March 2015 that featured nursing school graduates from universities across the state, Bentley turned to the nurses from UAB and quipped, "Do you guys have a football team up there?"

To the supporters of UAB, it all added another crimson log to their fire.

As they increased the pressure, Dr. Robert Witt, the chancellor of the UA System and previously president of the University of Alabama's main campus in Tuscaloosa, issued a statement to defend the board:

"During my nine years as President of the University of Alabama, I worked side-by-side with this Board of Trustees to help grow the campus and the System," Witt wrote. "There is no doubt that our governing structure and the synergies of UA, UAB and UAH are a point of tremendous pride for Alabama and a model for the nation. It is extremely unfortunate that a vocal few would choose to disagree."

In the end, was it as simple as an old grudge? Bartow had pushed for football against the wishes of Tuscaloosa leadership, and also in 1991 he had fired off a letter to the NCAA in which he accused several former Alabama coaches of cheating, after learning how to do so from Bryant himself. Was killing UAB football really just Paul Bryant Jr.'s final act before retiring from the UA Board of Trustees? Again, no one from the board would ever really acknowledge that question, and would it really matter if they did? Administrators could deny it, UAB supporters would believe what they wished to believe, and to them, the dots were all too easy to connect even if there were no clean, straight lines.

The perceptions were reality to those who picked up the fight.

"It was an old, old, old argument between Bear and Bartow," said UAB supporter Dr. Kristie Rankin. "And the fact that UAB was never supposed to have a football team, it was understood that you weren't going to have a football team, and you were not supposed to compete with the University of Alabama. The fact that UAB dared want a football team, it became ugly. So they killed it when they thought they could get away with it."

If so, the powers-that-be waited too long.

"There's an underbelly to this story that goes far deeper," veteran TV announcer Tim Brando said. "This wasn't just about economics. This was about a three-decades-long vendetta that Bryant Jr. had with Gene Bartow. ... I don't think that they ever thought there would be this kind of grassroots financial support."

The administration clearly was prepared for a shutdown. It was not prepared for the aftermath.

"If they had done this in 2013, right after Garrick McGee quit, nobody probably would have made much of a fuss," BlazerTalk's Paul Ensign said. "We were beaten down. People were tired. But Bill Clark brought back hope."

Bill Clark woke up the dragons. And the dragons were filled with a righteous fury that could burn the sun.

12

Chapter

Free UAB

Soon after the crowd dispersed and the television cameras had gone away—and with recruiters from other college teams literally already on their way to the UAB campus to recruit the now former Blazers—Timothy Alexander rolled into Bill Clark's office.

"Coach, I'm going to fight to get this program back," Timothy told him on that fateful December day. "I'm not going to stop fighting until we get it back."

Timothy paused. Then he said something he would go on to say many times: "And when we get it back, we're going to be bowl eligible first year back."

The initial shock of the programs being terminated hit the community hard, especially those who had worn the green and gold.

"It felt like a kick in the gut," said UAB alumnus Ralph Harbison. "Why was nobody stepping in to help us? Why were people allowing their petty jealousies to end something that had enriched so many lives throughout the years?"

Watching online, early program star Josh Evans shook his head in disgust. Evans was one of the original Blazers and became the program's first NFL player, suiting up in the starting lineup for the Tennessee Titans in a Super Bowl.

"I was in tears," Evans recalled. "I thought about the guys, the opportunities that were being taken away. It was not just about football. Just look at my senior class. We've got Walt Maddox, the mayor of Tuscaloosa who could be governor some day. We've got doctors, lawyers, very productive men. I was upset that the kids were not going to get that same opportunity that changed our lives. A lot of guys I came in with, we didn't have a lot of options, but we made the most of our chance at UAB. I thought a lot about that. Our program turned out real good men.

"I didn't think they would shut it down until it was over with. I just thought it was talk because we heard that same talk the whole four years I was there. I was skeptical that it could come back after they took it away. But you never can underestimate the power of people. They fought."

They also had a battle cry: Free UAB.

*** *** ***

The Free UAB Movement actually had been first born in 2011 when trustees pulled the rug out from under UAB's attempt to build an on-campus stadium. The protests had led a small group to Tuscaloosa to protest. Emails and phone numbers were exchanged. Social media connections were made. These would grow invaluable as the movement grew up in the aftermath of Watts' announcement. It included students, alumni, former players and business leaders. It was, for lack of a better term, guerilla warfare. Combatants gathered on social media, in secret chat rooms, in restaurants, in hallways. They built messaging, raised money for commercials, ordered pizzas and had them delivered to protesters. They tweeted, hashtagged, called reporters and called radio shows. They marched. They lobbied. They did anything they could to keep the message going and the story from falling out of the headlines.

Timothy was out front every day.

"He would go door to door, passing out flyers," said Autumn Burnett, the former UAB track athlete who volunteered to work with Timothy through countless hours of physical therapy. He would put the message out on social media, 'This is what we're going to do, meet me here, we're going to shut this city down, we're gonna walk the streets and if the police come out here and get us, they'll just come out here and get us.

"He took that same mindset that he has every day about walking again, and he put it into protesting and into getting those teams back."

Timothy drew motivation from two sayings he holds dear.

"History goes to the students," he said. Students, such as Burnett, had brought him this far in his recovery. "Students were going to bring football, bowling and rifle back."

Another slogan was perfect for the task at hand: "My opposition is my inspiration."

Former players from the 2014 team did their part, too. On his wrist for every game as an All-Big Ten running back for the Indiana Hoosiers, and then as an All-Pro rookie running back with the NFL's Chicago Bears, Jordan Howard wore a green jelly bracelet just like Timothy Alexander wore. In gold letters were two words: "Free UAB."

"We literally had nothing left to lose," said Chuck Tuggle, one of the founders of the original club team that launched football at UAB in 1989. "The team was gone."

Perhaps UAB football needed to die, some felt.

Photo courtesy of Dr. John Knox

The decision to eliminate the UAB football, bowling and rifle programs led to protests across campus, including a sign aimed at the UAB president next to a statue of program founder Gene Bartow at Bartow Arena.

There was a discussion to be had about how to best support it and meet institutional goals. There was no denying that the financial and on-the-field results for the program had been poor. Some people believed UAB would be better off to go back to its roots—basketball—and focus on sports where the school could be more successful. In fact, when it killed the programs, the administration announced that it didn't plan to cut the athletics budget. Instead, existing resources would be redeployed to sports in which it was believed UAB could be nationally competitive, such as basketball and soccer.

But that should have been a community decision, critics argued. No one asked.

"It had never been allowed to succeed," said Dr. John Knox, the former Rhodes Scholar finalist from the UAB Honors Program. "If you are set up to fail, *of course* you are not going to have success like you would if everyone is pulling together."

Now they were pulling together. And to understand why this passion burned bright, one must understand that it was not just about a football team. It was about self-determination and who would control the vision for the university. Knox was one of many UAB supporters who feared that dismantling athletics was just the beginning of a larger movement to dismantle the undergraduate programs at UAB, with the goal of shifting resources to the Tuscaloosa campus while refocusing UAB's mission toward graduate students and the medical school. He took this message so seriously that he went to see a former UA trustee, who, Knox claimed in commentary he wrote for several online publications, confirmed his worst fears.

This idea may have seemed outlandish to those not familiar with the dynamics involved, but it permeated the response of UAB supporters.

Alex Jones, who served as a talk-show host on the student-run Blaze Radio, said this was the talk of the campus in December 2014.

"You had to worry if this was going to be the start of the fall of all the undergraduate programs at UAB," Jones said. "You had professors worried about keeping their jobs. One of my friends was in the band and he was worried about what was going to happen to his scholarship. It was not just that football had been taken away but that so many people were going to be affected by it. People were concerned this was just the start."

As revolutions go, if Boston had its Tea Party, then Birmingham now had Free UAB. A fan even made a flag modeled after the famous "Gadsden Flag" of the Revolutionary War. Above the words, "DON'T TREAD ON ME," a dragon head inspired by the Blazer mascot had replaced the head of the iconic rattlesnake.

"Free UAB means so many things to me," said Dr. Kristie Rankin, a former UAB police officer who held degrees from both UAB and UA. "It means that we aren't anybody's second choice. We are not anybody's little sister. We are not an afterthought. Free UAB means that we control our own destiny. Free UAB means that we have the right to say what is good for UAB. Free UAB means that you should consult the alumni before you make decisions for the university. Free UAB means that UAB should be able to grow and expand. It means not just a football program. It means that UAB should not be harnessed on what it can accomplish by what the University of Alabama or anybody in state government thinks it should be able to accomplish."

It wasn't so much that the program was killed that animated this movement. It was *how* it was killed.

"Their first mistake was underestimating us," Rankin continued. "They thought they had more money, more power and that they could scare us. They thought we would get tired, we would get bored and we would go away. They underestimated our tenacity, they underestimated our loyalty and they damn sure underestimated our intelligence and resourcefulness."

If you were to make a Mount Rushmore of Free UAB leaders, one might start with Bill Clark himself. He sparked the rebellion simply by his success, but he threw his one and only public bomb at a ceremony honoring him for winning the Conference USA Coach of the Year award. As he left the stage, he paused. With eyes ablaze as if talking to his own team at halftime of a championship game, he delivered the mic drop that inspired a second wind. "Y'all don't stop giving them hell," the coach said. They didn't.

Such a monument might include Jack Williams, the Republican state representative from Vestavia Hills who picked up the legislative fight when others told him it was a lost cause, vowing to fight the "Jihad that had been waged against UAB." Or Justin Craft, the former UAB player who had become a rising star in the Birmingham business community and had beaten the Blazer drum among Birmingham's corporate power players.

There were countless others, some out front and some in the shadows. They worked non-stop for months.

And then there was Timothy Alexander.

There was no one more essential to the Free UAB Movement, and the effort to restore the UAB football, bowling and rifle programs — don't forget, UAB eliminated two other programs, much less conspicuously but no less painfully for the participants — than Timothy Alexander. The young man in the wheelchair simply would not stand down.

"I think in many ways he was the face of the return of UAB football," said Gene Hallman, chief executive officer of the Birmingham-based Bruno Event Team, a leading sports-events marketing firm. "Here is a student-athlete in Timothy who is obviously dealing with his handicap in a very positive way. I really believe people saw his perseverance and determination and here it was translated into a group as a whole that wasn't going to take no for an answer. They said, 'We're going to get our football program back.' People listened."

"You can't overstate it," Clark said. "He was the

voice when there was no voice. This was the voice of the student-athlete and the voice of the regular students who probably didn't feel like they had a voice."

"That young man inspires me on a daily basis," said Sirius XM college football analyst Rachel Baribeau. "He has reasons considering his health and what happened to him to be sad or to feel sorry for himself, but I have never seen him where he doesn't have a magnetic smile on his face from ear to ear. He is so inspiring. He literally is a magnet who draws people to him.

"He did everything he could to carry this message forward, and I just love him for that."

"Timothy Alexander is the human statue to the success of UAB—a statue with a pulse," Fox Sports broadcaster Tim Brando said. "Energy and enthusiasm and love and passion resonate with him."

His football coach at Erwin High School, Willie Miller, had seen that before. And he knew what was coming from Timothy.

"The people who shut down UAB football didn't know who they were dealing with," Miller said. "It took the heart of an individual who had accomplished things when everything was stacked against him. And Timothy knows the difference between right and wrong. If he knew something was right in his heart, there was nothing you were going to say that was going to change his mind.

"When you've got somebody who has beaten the odds like Tim, when he gets something in his head, something that he believes in and thinks is right, he's not going to stop. He's a bulldog. He's a fighter. He is not going to stop until you convince him otherwise. You might convince him, but you are going to have to convince him because he will stand up for what he believes."

13

Chapter

Hail Mary

In many ways, Timothy Alexander's story *was* the UAB football story.

Timothy began with such big dreams, only to have everything stripped away and be told those dreams were impossible. He had to reinvent himself into someone different, someone *better*. Someone who would never stop fighting to achieve things no one else believed possible. Someone who would not take no for an answer. Someone who wouldn't allow his possibilities to be defined by those who didn't share his vision.

He was at a university where the most famous quote by its first president, Dr. Joseph Volker, read simply: "We would do Birmingham a great disservice if we dream too little dreams."

Timothy was the poster for that quote.

When he met with former UAB coach Garrick McGee to discuss his dream — the most vivid dream he could imagine — of a kid in a wheelchair being on a college football team, all he asked for was an opportunity. Timothy told the coach he would become one of the greatest tight ends ever to play for UAB.

Now he was in the game. Timothy Alexander might never catch a pass in a game for the UAB Blazers, but he was going to complete a Hail Mary. He was going to bring UAB football — and bowling and rifle — back from the dead.

Timothy's first task was to rally and organize the students. He worked with friends, supporters and the student government association to create a group he called Free UAB Student Organization, or FUSO for short. They made banners and t-shirts. Timothy researched the economic impact of the university on the city of Birmingham and the state. He researched the civic contributions and career achievements of UAB foot-

Photo courtesy of Free UAB Student Organization
Timothy Alexander leads a student protest during a UAB basketball game in 2014, two days after the Blazer football, bowling and rifle programs were eliminated.

ball players across the state. From that, Timothy created a list of talking points that he and others would use in interviews or whenever they spoke to a crowd. Students were mobilized at a moment's notice for protest marches. A network of contacts was built, including students, alumni, civic leaders, politicians and friends of the program. People who had never before met or spoken to each other now were connecting across social media, building alliances and coordinating their message.

Timothy sought out mentors—people who could help him with speeches, with organizational tactics, with research or resources and to counsel him on how to speak to different groups with different messages. One minute he might be speaking to a lawyer, the next to a reporter, and then minutes later to a student.

The resistance had multiple fronts: Protests, social media activism, information distribution, media outreach, political lobbying, community involvement and, finally, fundraising. It was a simple message. They would show how UAB football was one of the university's best assets. They would demonstrate the numbers in the study used to eliminate the football program were flawed. They would show support both in numbers and dollars. They would communicate how the program increased value—in quantifiable and intangible ways—for both the university and a Birmingham region that was in an important period of economic renaissance. And they would point to successful case studies at comparable universities where investment in football had paid big dividends. It made no sense for the state's largest employer and one of its leading economic drivers to eliminate one of the most cost-effective ways to engage and promote the community.

"What's good for UAB is good for Birmingham and is good for Alabama," said Justin Craft, the former player who was one of the program's leading advocates.

Anytime and anywhere there were news cameras, one probably could find Timothy Alexander.

One of the first big moments came on December 4, two days after the football program's demise. Hundreds of UAB students, dressed in black, marched on the campus green outside Bartow Arena before a UAB basketball game. They held candles. They sang songs. They prayed. Key community leaders spoke.

Photo courtesy of Free UAB Student Organization

Timothy Alexander speaks to assembled UAB supporters on the steps of the Alabama state capitol in Montgomery.

Leading them from his wheelchair, megaphone in hand, was Timothy Alexander.

"We're fixing to make a UAB movement tonight," Timothy told the crowd. "We're just making a stand. There comes a time when you have to make a stand."

They chanted, "We want football! We want football!" They chanted "Free UAB!" There were battle cries, including one chant that followed the basketball team all the way to run to the Conference USA Tournament championship and an upset of third-seeded Iowa State in the NCAA Tournament in March:

"Fire Ray Watts!"

"We're going to make our opinions known," Timothy said. "We're going to make our feelings known, and we're going to free UAB."

It became a hashtag: #FreeUAB.

"We made it trend worldwide," Timothy said.

Social media was a key battle ground, one the administration "didn't understand and didn't know how to fight," according to UAB alumnus Ralph Harbison. All the expensive New York crisis management firms in the world were a step behind what was happening on the ground, and in cyberspace, in Birmingham, Alabama.

"Social media—hashtag activism—is what saved UAB football," Harbison said. "If it had not been for social media, our ability to get the message out, stay ahead of the message, contact each other, it wouldn't have been possible. We were able to communicate in real time."

Timothy was everywhere in the winter and spring of 2015, always with a smile and a message.

It took him to the capitol of Alabama, Montgomery, where he and dozens of other UAB supporters lobbied legislators and spoke on the steps of the capitol building. It took him to towns large and small across Alabama. Multiple times per week, Timothy would load his wheelchair into Thanasis Nicolau's handicap-accessible van and criss-cross the metro Birmingham area to visit city council meetings and ask them to pass resolutions supporting the return of the UAB football, bowling and rifle programs.

"He was just awesome," said Phyllis Aderholt Rodgers, a UAB alumnus and football supporter who helped organize UAB fans to accompany Timothy to those meetings. "Everything he did, he was so determined to bring it back and to not give up. Tim was just

Timothy Alexander's travels across the state of Alabama to promote the return of UAB football, bowling and rifle meant many nights of studying and speech-writing while on the road inside Thanasis Nicolau's van.

such a motivator and go-getter. He rallied everybody."

By the time late spring arrived in 2015, the efforts had produced more than 50 resolutions across the state, as far as two hours from Birmingham.

"He was going to some places I never even heard of," said his UAB football teammate, Tristan Henderson. "He was reaching out to places that people just pass through. He just said, 'I am going to reach out to every single person, every single soul, and I am going to tell them what is going on at UAB and I am going to convince them to sign a petition to get it back on the right track.'"

Timothy juggled class assignments with speaking engagements, all the while working the phones and social media accounts. He found ways to multi-task.

"I'd work on my speech in Thanasis' van on the drive up to wherever we were going," Timothy recalled. "I would study the community where we were going and find out things like whether there had ever been any UAB players from their schools. I would try to help them see that UAB football was important to their communities, too. Then on the drive back, I would study for my classes."

Nicolau, a Birmingham trial attorney and UAB alumnus, met Timothy at one of the first protests. He was impressed with his drive and attitude, and when Timothy asked him for help, he couldn't say no. He had special reason to marvel at Timothy's stamina and drive as well as specific understanding of some of his needs.

"My mother was paralyzed after an equestrian

accident and is in a wheelchair and I've been a caretaker for her," Nicolau said. "So I am very familiar with paralysis. I knew what Timothy was challenged with physically and mentally as he took on this fight.

"He made it look tireless every day. But it's not. You have to remember that Tim weighs 260 pounds. And he's just got his arms to move. He's got to get his whole body into a shower, crawl to dry himself off, crawl into his room to get his clothes, crawl to get dressed, get himself back up into a wheelchair. Just getting your pants on is hard. And a lot of people don't know, that with paralysis, he suffers from severe muscle spasms. He's doing stuff like it is nothing that a lot of people need assistance just to get out of their house.

"And then on top of all this, he's doing great work in school and the other things he was involved in."

Two weeks after the UAB football program was shut down, Timothy Alexander crossed paths again with Dr. Ray Watts, the man who had stood in front of the room and shattered his dreams.

This time, Timothy fulfilled another thing that at one time people told him would not be possible. He rolled across the stage in Bartow Arena, just a few feet from the spot where he had held his fist high in a protest. This time, it was a commencement ceremony. On December 13, 2014, Timothy Alexander earned a double bachelor's degree in Criminal Justice and Communication Studies. He shook Watts' hand as he accepted his diploma.

As he rolled his wheelchair off the stage, Timothy paused. He held a football— a UAB football—high above his head.

14

Chapter

The End Zone

Bringing UAB football back was not going to be easy. The administration had no real reason to reconsider. Even as the protests continued and the uproar rose to include votes of no confidence against Dr. Ray Watts, the UAB president, by students, faculty and alumni as well as calls for his resignation by politicians such as State Rep. Jack Williams, there was a presumption that the protests eventually would die down and the community would move on. UA System chancellor Robert Witt, in backing Watts, derisively called the protestors "the vocal few." It was a nickname that stuck like a badge of honor, but it didn't change one key fact:

"The odds were so stacked against UAB football coming back," said Steve Irvine, a longtime reporter covering UAB sports for The Birmingham News and 247Sports.com. "You had to have somebody who is just going to say, 'I am going to fight this every day.' I am sure there were days where even Bill Clark thought, 'I don't know if this is worth it.'

"But I don't think Tim Alexander ever had that

day where he said he could take a day off. I think he is unique in that. He just kept pounding and pounding, getting people at these meetings, getting people at these marches, making phone calls, just showing up. That's what he did. You don't win this fight without that person because it is a hard situation to keep fighting."

In early January 2015, Watts created a sliver of hope when he agreed to commission a second study to review the Carr Report, which had quickly been discredited by those who supported the program as a poorly conceived attempt to provide justification for a predetermined outcome.

"One of the biggest flaws was that it didn't take into account that if UAB drops football, they are most likely going to have to leave Conference USA and you are losing that revenue," said former CBSSports.com reporter Jon Solomon. "Conference USA had a bylaw that you had to play football. If UAB did not have football, they were not going to be in C-USA long term. That was never factored into the calculations.

"There were differences in how they counted football donations in their NCAA report and what Carr counted; I would annually get these financial reports, what Carr was putting in his report was different from what UAB was reporting. It clearly was skewed to show that football didn't have as many donations as UAB showed. They also just had a basic miscalculation on arithmetic, off by tens of thousands of dollars on one line. I remember bringing it to UAB and they were just like, 'good catch.' It really hurts your credibility when you are killing a program and you have basic arithmetic mistakes."

The movement continued. Polls conducted across the state showed 83 percent of voters favored reinstating the program. Timothy's campaign was beginning to rack up resolutions from major communities, particularly Birmingham's affluent suburbs such as Homewood, Hoover and Vestavia Hills. Rep. Jack Williams introduced legislation to restore the football program and restructure the UA System Board of Trustees.

And then on March 23, Williams unveiled a bombshell: Documents he claimed showed the administration had been planning a shutdown since before Clark had coached his first game in 2014. He called for Watts' immediate resignation.

Yes, momentum was clearly on Free UAB's side. A new study found that UAB football had not been as financially strained as previously reported, and that realistic projections and modest investment could give it a chance to be viable. Negotiations began to define how much money would actually be required to reinstate the programs. A new athletics director, Mark Ingram from Temple University, was hired. A pledge drive was begun. Season ticket deposits were taken.

Further, a negative impact from the decision began to emerge. Enrollment went down for the first time in years and donations to a $1 billion capital campaign slowed dramatically as alumni mailed in their pledge cards with the phrase #notanotherdime.

Then most importantly, inspired by the protests

and awakened to the potential, Birmingham's business community stepped up. A May 2015 meeting of prominent Birmingham business leaders quickly raised pledges for millions of dollars over a five-year-period. The students at UAB passed a resolution to raise fees to contribute $550,000 annually to the programs. The City of Birmingham pledged $2.5 million over five years. All told, pledges eventually would come in at more than $48 million, including $22 million for a state-of-the-art practice facility, if the programs were brought back.

June 1, 2015 was to be decision day.

Timothy was nervous all day. Everything that could be done had been done. All the marches, all the letters, all the prayers had come to this day. They gathered outside the administration building on 20th Street on the UAB campus on the south side of Birmingham,

Photo courtesy of Raycom Sports

Timothy Alexander watches a television outside the UAB Administration Building as he awaits an announcement by Dr. Ray Watts about the possible reinstatement of the UAB football, bowling and rifle programs.

hundreds of them now all familiar to each other — a family, the UAB Family, as they called themselves — to the same place where the first protest had launched their fight. They were dressed in green and gold. They waved flags and held signs. The marching band played.

They greeted each other with words. "Ever faithful!" someone would shout. "Ever loyal!" would be the reply.

Those words meant everything to Timothy Alexander.

"'Ever faithful, ever loyal,' is UAB's creed," Timothy explained. "It's the language that we talk to family through, to be ever faithful and ever loyal no matter what we're going through in life. That really hits home with me. One of my favorite passages that I've ever read says that but without faith it's impossible to please God and it is impossible to do anything, and that faith without works is dead, so you've got to be ever faithful and ever loyal every single day. You've got to wake up and be disciplined. You've got to commit and be consistent. That is what 'ever faithful, ever loyal' means to me."

Timothy huddled the crowd up for a prayer and a pep talk. This was either going to be the biggest celebration yet—or the biggest protest yet.

For Timothy, this battle had never been personal. He truly believed that eventually the UAB administration would come to realize a mistake had been made and that it could be made right. Dr. John Knox, the former UAB Honors Program student and Rhodes Scholar finalist, remained skeptical. Dressed in the same blue suit and crimson UA tie he had worn to trustee meetings to mock the UAB president, Knox shook a blue water bottle as Watts had done during the shutdown meeting in December 2014 and confessed that he would believe UAB football was coming back when he heard those words from Watts himself.

While even some of the most passionate Blazer fans had not seen much hope for victory in the beginning, Timothy had made plenty of believers during these seven months.

"At first, I wasn't so sure," said Autumn Burnett, the physical therapist who had trained alongside Timothy when he was a member of the UAB football team. "But after seeing the dedication and the passion that

Photo courtesy of Raycom Sports

As he hears the good news, Timothy Alexander celebrates the reinstatement of the UAB football, bowling and rifle programs on June 1, 2015.

Tim protested with, after seeing Tim being Tim at his finest, I believed. He was like the Martin Luther King Jr. of UAB football."

Inside the building, Dr. Ray Watts stepped to the podium under the lights, with thousands watching on Birmingham television and fans and alumni scattered as far away as Antarctica watching online. Timothy and the rest watched on a television from the sidewalk below.

"Given the broad base of support never before seen, as of today, we are taking steps to reinstate the football, rifle and bowling programs," the UAB president began …

Timothy didn't hear the rest. He closed his eyes and turned his face to the sky as his arms rose above his head. Soon, pundits on the television would be analyzing what had just happened.

"I've never seen anything quite like this," Paul Finebaum, a longtime Birmingham media personality who had moved on to the SEC Network, said on ESPN. "The people won. The little people, the average guy in the street. Joe Schmoe was finally heard.

"The president made a terrible decision. He opened the door for every conspiracy theorist in the world. I haven't heard this many conspiracies since Dealy Plaza in 1963. Everyone stood up for this program and they became America's team and I think finally the guys in the blue suits, the people in the ivory towers, listened."

Timothy didn't hear that, either. Surrounded

by the celebrating mob, he collapsed his head onto the shoulder of Kimberly Craft, the wife of Justin Craft who had been so instrumental in making this day happen, too. And they cried the sweetest tears imaginable as the celebration erupted and the flags were waved.

Timothy's muscular arms are covered with tattoos. Each has meaning. In ink on his left wrist are three words: God is faithful.

God had been faithful. UAB football was coming back.

15

Chapter

Keep On Trucking

There was so much to do. UAB would be creating a football program from scratch to compete immediately in the FBS as a member of Conference USA. A new contract would need to be negotiated for Bill Clark, who turned down opportunities elsewhere to lead this revival. There was a new hashtag: #TheReturn. Players had to be recruited, all that money had to be collected and shovels had to go into the ground soon on an innovative covered practice facility and football operations center. Literally every aspect of the program would have to start over. The vast majority of the players were gone. Heck, even most of the equipment was, too.

A timetable was set: UAB would return to the football field on September 2, 2017. More than 1,000 days would pass between that date and the previous time a collection of Blazers had taken the field. It seemed light years in the distance yet it would be upon them so quickly. There was so much to do. "Unprecedented," athletic director Mark Ingram often liked to say. Yes, nobody had ever really tried to kill their football program and bring it back from the dead a few months later.

Timothy Alexander, of course, was going to be right in the middle of it. Clark had a special role for Timothy: Director of Character Development. He would be in charge of relations with former players and in creating opportunities for community service for the UAB football team. This would come on the heels of a remarkable academic achievement. One year after Timothy walked across a stage to earn a double bachelor's degrees in Criminal Justice and Communications Studies, he would complete the work for a master's degree while leading the rally for the return of the program.

To his friends, this might have been his biggest achievement yet.

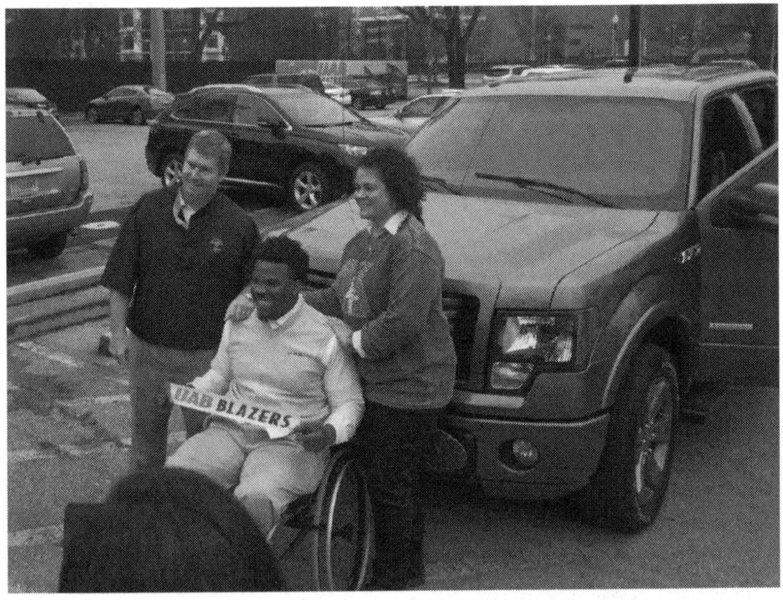

Photo courtesy of Patricia Alexander

Justin and Kim Craft present Timothy Alexander with a new handicap-accessible truck after UAB fans conducted a Secret Santa fundraising collection to purchase it for Timothy.

"The amazing thing to me, when Tim was in the car wreck, he didn't just have the spinal injury," said Thanasis Nicolau, the trial attorney who had mentored Timothy during all those visits to city councils. "He had a brain injury. He had to teach himself how to feed himself, how to read again, how to speak again. He had a lot of learning difficulties that he had to power through just to be able to get back into school."

The following Monday, there was a surprise waiting.

On the morning of December 17, 2015, Timothy rolled his wheelchair out of the UAB football office to find a crowd of dozens of familiar faces in the same parking lot where protesters had cursed Ray Watts and cried out in agony at the loss of their team. His mother Patricia was there, along with other family members. Bishop Stephen Davis, from Timothy's church, was there. Lauren Sisler, the television reporter from the local CBS affiliate who had done the first news story on Timothy back in 2013, was there.

"Merry Christmas!" they yelled.

Justin and Kim Craft smiled. Then Justin handed Timothy a set of keys.

In the space where Timothy had held his special cleats and cried about the loss of the UAB program sat a new handicap-accessible, charcoal gray Ford F-150 pickup truck with black interior and a wheelchair lift. It had a personalized university tag: UABFAM. And it was now his. Free and clear. Friends, family, alumni and supporters had chipped in $5 or $25 or $100 or

$1,000 at a clip to purchase the vehicle for Timothy as a Christmas gift. It was the most marvelous Secret Santa gesture imaginable.

Tears flowed again. This was the UAB Family's way to take care of someone who had given so much of himself without ever asking for a thing in return.

"Tim showed the love for this place, just the pure love. No other reason, "said 247Sports.com reporter Steve Irvine. "That's important, the message of persistence. His persistence, how he's lived his life, is the key to all this."

For Sisler, there to cover the story, it was one of those moments where the objectivity of a journalist collides with the emotions of the human spirit. She remembered a college kid in a wheelchair approaching her one day at a UAB sporting event and saying he'd someday be on the football team. A year later, he was on that team and she was the first reporter to tell the story of the persistent young man with a big smile and a bigger heart.

"There aren't enough words to describe Timothy Alexander," Sisler said. "He is somebody that when you see him, you just want to drop everything and give him a hug. You want to embrace him. He embraces life like nobody I have ever seen before or anybody I have ever met. He has taken his situation and turned it into something extremely positive and is impacting more people than he will ever know. Throughout this entire journey, he has stayed humble. He is using his circumstance for the greater good. That is one of life's greatest rewards, and he has taught me that.

"He is a big reason why I love my job. Not because of the wins and losses. Not because I am out on the football field when the confetti falls after the national championship. It is the people like Timothy Alexander."

There was another big moment in Timothy's life before the Blazers returned to the field.

She had caught his attention in 2014. The UAB football players were hanging around in Bartow Arena, waiting on a team meal, watching the women's basketball team practice.

"I saw this basketball shoot across the court," Timothy remembered, "and I saw the most beautiful hand I had ever seen in my life reach out for the ball,

Photo courtesy of Tierra Andrews
On the same day she graduated from UAB, Kayla Bryant, right, is all smiles after Timothy took a knee to propose marriage at the site of their first date. She said yes.

and I followed it up, and I was like, 'Oh my gosh.' I yelled out real loud, 'Fellas, I've got to have her.'"

Kayla Bryant was breathtaking.

One of the UAB coaches chided him. "Oh no, man of God, she's got both parents at home, she's got an awesome mom and dad, you're going to have to come at her correct," he told Timothy. They developed a friendship, but Timothy wanted more.

Photo courtesy of Kayla Bryant
Timothy and Kayla are making wedding plans for 2018, and Timothy is planning to walk his bride down the aisle.

"I was like, 'Listen, I want to be your friend, but I don't want to stay your friend. I like you.'" Her words to me were, 'I have never had a boyfriend and I am scared of what others might think if I date someone in a wheelchair."

'I said, 'You know what, it's your loss. I'm not worried about a girl, I'm worried about the right girl. If God starts to change your heart, don't run from it.' I asked her to be my girlfriend on May 1, 2014."

She was there by his side through all of the Free UAB movement. Now here he was on December 17, 2016, on her college graduation day, taking her for a celebratory luncheon at a barbecue restaurant near the UAB campus, site of their first date. With a bit of help from friends and two weeks of practice with his physical therapist, Timothy climbed out of his wheelchair and got down on bended knee. "Will you marry me?" he asked on the sidewalk as Kayla burst into tears.

To this day, the answer lights up his smile. In texts, he shares the news in capital letters:

"SHE SAID YES AFTER THE CAR WRECK!"

16

Chapter

The Return

It all was building up to this. September 2, 2017 at Legion Field, the UAB Blazers were going to run out of that tunnel to face the Alabama A&M Bulldogs. News outlets from across the country would be there. ESPN would do a special feature. Country music superstar Sam Hunt—a former UAB quarterback—would host a special free concert in front of more than 20,000 fans in downtown Birmingham the night before. The hype had been building for more than two years.

On this day, The Return got real.

For Timothy Alexander, gameday came with familiar feelings—the kind he had experienced as the star tight end for the Erwin Eagles 11 years before. He had responsibilities. He was all business. He had a new job with the UAB broadcast team, hosting part of the pregame show. And as UAB's Director of Character Development, his role during the game would be to help the Blazers focus between plays. Part cheerleader, part pastor, part guidance counselor, Timothy Alexander held tremendous influence with the young men in the green and gold.

But today there would be something more.

"Make sure you're in your seats about 30 minutes before kickoff," UAB athletic director Mark Ingram was telling fans at the various tailgate tents outside Legion Field. "There's something you're not going to want to miss. I don't think there will be a dry eye in the house."

That morning, Timothy went outside his apartment and soaked in the sun. He prayed. "God, thank you. Thank you for this opportunity. It's a big day today." He did the same when he arrived at Legion Field,

Photo courtesy UAB

Timothy Alexander promised that when UAB football returned, he would lead the Blazers out onto the field. He did so by walking the game ball to midfield, surrounded by his teammates from the 2014 squad.

touching the ground and praying over the turf. He told his fiance, Kayla, not to call him until it was over because he had to be focused. Just as the UAB football team had been practicing for two years for this day, so had Timothy.

Timothy thought of all the people he'd met on his journey. He thought of his physical therapists, including Natalia Shannon from Drayer Physical Therapy, who had seen him in a news story two years ago and taken him on as a client just as his insurance coverage had run out and his only help was the UAB football program and his volunteer friends. He thought of those who had inspired him, those who had doubted him. He thought about this place, Legion Field, where he dreamed he would one day play college football. It had been this place, after all, where he was en route to watch a football game on October 28, 2006, before his life changed forever in an instant.

He thought of his brother David, who on the day before he was killed in an automobile accident, had issued a challenge to Timothy about getting his life right: 'I want you to go to the NFL and make a great name for yourself, to take care of the community and the family,' David told him. "I love you." Those were David's last words to Timothy. He had never forgotten them. He carries them with him today.

While the players were going through their pregame preparations, so did Timothy. His heart was racing. His therapists greeted him. "It's here Tim, you did it!" someone said, but he brushed off congratulations.

He wasn't in the mood for rah-rah. He wanted to be calm and focused, he told them. "Calm mind, fast body, because what we're doing is bigger than me."

Timothy Alexander had on his game face. He had to guard against painful muscle spasms as they prepared for what was next. "One wrong breathing technique could have sent my whole body into spasms," he said.

Members of the 2014 UAB football team were lined up onto the field. With the new Blazers in the tunnel preparing to run onto the field, the game ball would first be delivered by the former players, a symbolic transfer of the old to the new. "It's game time!" someone said. A record crowd for a UAB football game, 45,212 fans, was filling into the stands at historic Legion Field. Timothy tuned out the crowd as he moved into position.

With Timothy's legs now fitted into braces, his therapists lifted him out of his wheelchair at the 40-yard line. Huddled around him were players, administrators, cheerleaders, referees. Timothy Alexander was keeping his promise. Timothy was leading the Blazers onto the field.

With his therapists close by to keep him steady, Timothy swayed his body to shift his weight. He was in agony, but forward he went as the muscles in his abdomen created the momentum that propelled his legs ahead. Two steps. Three steps. He fought back the pain. Four steps. Five. The crowd began to understand what was happening as Timothy's image appeared on the stadium's video board. There were audible gasps. Then cheers. Thunderous cheers.

"Go Tim!" some shouted. Grown men cried like babies. Another step, then another, then another.

Months of grueling two-hour training, including 21 straight days in August, prepared him for this moment. Eleven years after tragedy took the use of his legs, with 10 yards covered and with his body feeling as if on fire, Timothy Alexander kissed the game ball and lifted it above his head at midfield.

"To God be the glory!" he thought as he passed it to the officials and those around him slapped his back.

UAB would go on to win the game 38-7, capping a spectacular day to launch what would become a spectacular season for a team that had been ranked dead last in the national rankings in the preseason. The Blazers had t-shirts made that said "No. 130" on the front, and "They don't know," on the back as a reminder of where they started. The Blazers would win seven more times. They would astound the college football world by finishing second in Conference USA's Western Division. They would beat three teams that went to bowl games. They would finish undefeated at home. They would lead Conference USA in attendance for the season, averaging more than 26,000 fans per game. Bill Clark would be named national coach of the year by several publications.

And they fulfilled Timothy's promise to Coach Clark back on the day UAB football was left for dead: They qualified for a bowl game their first season back.

But in a season filled with unforgettable memories, one set the tone for it all. Another promise kept.

Timothy Alexander had — literally — carried UAB football back home.

"Tim walking to midfield was the exclamation point for The Return," said Jordan Howard, Timothy's Blazer teammate in 2014 who went on to be a star running back for the NFL's Chicago Bears.

"It was breathtaking," Timothy would say later of how he felt at midfield. "We did it. It was one of the greatest moments of my life."

It was a moment would go viral on Twitter. It would be featured on ESPN's SportsCenter. It would be viewed millions of times on websites and on social media.

Van Phillips, the principal at Erwin High School where Tim had been a football star before the accident, was one of those viewers who soaked in each step. As someone who had been there from the start of the journey, it was an overwhelming scene.

"It brought tears to my eyes," Phillips said. "What I saw was a young man who could have given up on life, could have sat by the side of the road the rest of his life and been angry and never come outside again. He could have taken the attitude that life had given him a bad deal and been angry with God."

Timothy's journey to that moment became a lesson in Phillips' school.

"The theme of our school this year is, 'We Won,'" Phillips said. "And there are four parts to it: We came.

We saw. We conquered. And we won. With that first step that he took, Tim came. He came to understand who he was, and where he was. He saw. He saw opportunities that there is a road in life, and he can go left or right, he can go right or wrong, I can go the dark side or the light side, and he chose the light side.

"He came, he saw, and then he conquered. He conquered all of the demons that were against him, he conquered all the naysayers who didn't give a second chance, he may have even conquered his own mind that told him he couldn't do this or that. And the last, Tim won. He came, he saw, he conquered and he won. And it wasn't just a win for the past. He's winning every day. For every person who sees darkness, Tim is a ray of hope."

17

Chapter

A New Mission

Timothy Alexander had accomplished so much. He had even won an Emmy Award for his work with a team of students who worked with Raycom Sports to produce a documentary film about the fight to save the UAB football program. But it wasn't in his nature to rest. There was so much more he wanted to do. Like everything, Timothy had a plan. He speaks it into believing, and then into being. Everyone else he comes into contact with seems to come along for the ride.

"Tim is the epitome of endurance, consistency and the strong will to accomplish the things in life that he sets out to do," said Bishop Stephen A. Davis, pastor of New Birth Birmingham, where Timothy attends church and leads the youth group every Tuesday.

It was Bishop Davis who had reached Timothy during that Sunday sermon, where Timothy arrived at church still in the clothes he had worn to the club the night before and was a lost young man trying to sort out what kind of life he could have in a wheelchair.

"Regardless of where a person is or what they

are going through, I still see potential," Bishop Davis said. "I still saw potential in Tim even when he was going through things as a teen. I still saw potential after the accident. I must minister to the potential in a person, not the condition that they are in. Tim grabbed ahold of that message that day."

In time, Timothy learned to grab strength from how his message could inspire others.

"I knew that my life was a 'Show Me' life," he said. "People have got to see me in the wheelchair, see the physical pain, see what I've been through. When someone sees it and is inspired by it, that's my healing process."

Some have even said Timothy Alexander could keep another promise: To be the greatest football player in UAB history. And when you think about that, he certainly could become the most influential player ever, even though he never took a snap in a game. Because the man in the wheelchair stood up for three programs, literally thousands of young men – and women – will receive college educations through their participation in UAB sports. Someday in the distant future, Timothy Alexander will return to a UAB football stadium and in the stands will be doctors, lawyers, teachers, coaches and more who benefitted through their participation and gave back in their own way.

"I believe if you can help someone connect their heart and their mind, they can accomplish anything they want in this life," Timothy said. "Ten years from now, this story will be known as a young man who helped save UAB football, but not just that, he left a legacy. He did run out of the tunnel. He did help save three programs and because of a guy that led this fight, people will be able to go to school through athletics at UAB. We will never have to worry about it being shut down again. A guy who helped raise $48 million and never asked for anything."

Timothy speaks often about adding value to others. This philosophy makes him appealing to anyone he meets. His ability to make a connection with any group, any age, any demographic has some people believing he could become a pastor or a coach or a motivational speaker. Some even believe he could have a future in politics. Governor Alexander? He isn't thinking that way now, but should he ever set his mind to it, there would be little reason to doubt, would there?

"Tim believes he can encourage young people, middle-aged people, elderly people, regardless of whatever arena he is in," Bishop Davis said. "He walks in as a light."

As a speaker, Timothy makes a dramatic impression.

"There's never been a time where I have not left his presence and not been ten times better," said Sirius XM college football analyst Rachel Baribeau. "I leave his presence and I feel like I have gotten a shot of all that is good in the world."

Baribeau had gotten to know Timothy during the football shutdown when she served as a coach for an alumni flag football game that was a de facto spring game for the dormant program in April 2015. It was a true rallying cry for the Blazers' fan base at a time when it was by no means certain UAB football would return. As the clock wound down, teammates wanted her to call a play for Timothy. In the shadow of the bleachers where his 2014 UAB teammates had taken him to the top of the stadium, this time the entire collection of former players—ranging from alumni from 1991 to 2014—pushed him into the end zone for the winning touchdown.

"I will never forget it," Baribeau said. "It was such a special moment."

"I don't know how he did it," she continued. "With God's grace and fortitude, that's how he did it. The mission he was on was almost superhuman. He never had a tired moment where he said, 'I just can't,' or 'I am not feeling well today' or 'I can't get there.' He always just found a way."

Timothy now speaks to colleges, high schools, middle schools and elementary schools across the nation. Companies bring him in as a motivational speaker, too. As a young man, he had seen the inside of a cell. Now he was counseling and praying with young men and women in jail—young men and women who probably were similar to the angry Timothy Alexander of his teenage years.

"Now I go back to the juvenile centers, I go back to the prisons and I share with people that you don't have to be a product of your environment," Timothy said. "You can change. I was a product of my environment, but now I am a guy that made it out. I changed my influence. I never got into any more trouble.

"I don't run or hide from my story. Yes, I was a juvenile delinquent. That's why I can relate to people that the world can't. I have walked in their shoes."

That message strikes a chord with Officer Ali Daniels, the officer who set Timothy on a better path with a man-to-man talk in the back of a police car.

"Timothy's message is very powerful," Daniels said. "I am so proud of him. The thing I love about it is his message is multicultural. It's not just black children, not just white children. His message reaches out to the masses."

Timothy's transformation from troubled teen to inspirational man didn't happen overnight. His uncle, Wayne Woolf, was there to witness it.

"The Lord took Tim's legs so that he could live," Woolf said. "Tim wasn't the model child. I feel like the Lord took his legs to save his life. If that wouldn't have happened the way it happened, we might not have Tim today. He was a rough kid. He got in trouble. To look at him now, you wouldn't believe it. It is why I get so choked up when I talk about him. I just want to holler and scream and thank God. It wasn't nothing but God."

The angry young man first walked in faith. He regained use of his upper body. In 2016, he stood brief-ly for the first time in 10 years, steps that gave him the confidence and courage to pursue his goal of walking the Blazers out onto Legion Field.

"I made peace with God when I saw my dreams

start coming true," Timothy said. "I went at Him through faith and started showing and seeing what would happen if someone just believed and trusted in Him. We've been best friends ever since.

"I pay attention to my body, so when these little signs of wonder started coming back, I was very excited and I just wanted to keep going after God. I understood that my story would be one of the great underdog stories."

What would the 15-year-old Timothy Alexander, the one on the path to prison, think of the man he would see today?"

"He would look himself in the mirror and say, 'I'm proud of you,'" Timothy said. "'I believe you'll go farther and do more.' You know, I never see the glass half-full or half-empty. I am just thankful for the glass. I just want to get the most I can out of life.

"(When I was in high school), I would have record-breaking games and great accomplishments and my brother would always talk about what I didn't do right and push me to be better because you never want to get complacent in life. You can be content, but you should never be complacent. I truly believe the 15-year-old Timothy Alexander would tell me to keep going because you are changing lives and that I have a role model I can look up to."

Timothy's story includes making peace with his father, Marvin, who now lives with him and is suffering from memory issues as he grows older. Timothy is now in the caretaker role, working to build a relationship where a void had been. His parents divorced when he was 5, and Patricia believes her son's longing for a deeper relationship with his father fueled his teenage rebellion, and that feelings of rejection led Timothy to direct that anger at her. Timothy doesn't see it exactly that way, but he does now have an opportunity to make up for lost time. The man in the wheelchair, at one time "so helpless that I was like a baby," now takes care of someone who cannot fully care for himself.

"I used to be mad that my dad wasn't there," Timothy said, "but whenever I really needed something, he was there. Every time I see him, I have mixed feelings but I can't relay all my feelings. I just have to do what God would do. I just wanted to know why, but now I know why—his father wasn't there for him. Like the other day, I was cooking for him, and he said, 'I see I taught you some things,' and I am like, 'You didn't teach me nothing.' But I love my dad. I don't reflect on him not being there. I am just happy he is in my life now and we are making memories. It sucks that he wasn't at my graduation and it sucks that we didn't do some things and it sucks that I only saw him on weekends. I didn't choose any of that. He chose it. But when I did need him, he was there."

Someday he hopes to take care of his mother, Patricia, too. The tough times of his teenage years have been replaced by admiration and respect for the single mother who worked tirelessly and went through so much to raise Timothy into the man he is today.

"She was tough as a bull with a heart full of

love," Timothy said. "We didn't really do a lot of hugging because she had to raise three young men on her own. She's been through a lot. She always talked about giving, giving our last to someone else. She didn't play. I am strong because my mother is strong. I never saw her cry in front of me. I heard her cry out to God in her bedroom, but she never cried in front of me. My brother is 6-foot-10 and I saw her stand up on a chair and go upside his head. She would fight us like a man. She didn't play. She loved God. She got up every day before the sun came up to pray. She is my inspiration.

"My mother has been working a minimum wage job for about 27 years, just to provide. I pray that one day I will make enough to retire my mom."

His former principal at Erwin High, Van Phillips, beams with pride when he discusses Tim's educational accomplishments, especially considering that at one time after the accident, doctors were unsure Timothy would be able to talk or read because of his brain injuries.

"My heart jumps out like he's an adopted son of mine, and it just shows what perseverance and surrounding yourself with people who are cheerleaders for you and keep you on that straight and narrow path can do," Phillips said. "People who pour into you and they don't take away from you. I told Tim one day, 'It's a God thing, it's not a Tim thing anymore.'"

Timothy dreams of creating his own foundation, of creating schools that help at-risk children to make better choices, providing them with life skills to complement academic skills. He wants to become a renowned motivational speaker, something that would surprise no one who has ever heard him speak.

"It all comes so naturally to him," Thanasis Nicolau, one of his mentors, said. "He is a great speaker."

Timothy is already on his way as a motivational speaker. He is partnered with an Atlanta-based organization called Growing Leaders, touring the country speaking to colleges as large as the University of Michigan — where he posed for photos with Wolverines football coach Jim Harbaugh and basketball coach John Beilien — to small elementary schools. He even could be seen speaking to junior-college football players on the popular Nexflix documentary series, "Last Chance U."

Bob Billings met Timothy at a Growing Leaders conference in December 2015; they were seated at a table next to each other. In his role as director of student support and partnerships for the Greeley-Evans Weld County School District in Colorado, he immediately began making plans for Timothy to visit. It led to Timothy's first paid speaking engagement, and since then he has made multiple appearances at schools and universities all across northern Colorado at Billings' request.

"Timothy has a profound message and larger-than-life personality," Billings said. "Whenever you are doing leadership development and bringing in leadership, one of hardest things to do is to measure outcomes that go along with that. Timothy has been in 10 or 12 different schools here over last two years. His personality is infectious, his story is inspiring and he just draws people to his presence."

An appearance at Northridge High School partic-

Photo courtesy of the University of Michigan

Timothy Alexander now speaks to college teams across the country, such as the Michigan Wolverines football team of coach Jim Harbaugh (left), and the basketball team coached by John Beilein (not pictured).

ularly caught Billings' attention.

"I had someone tell me, 'I have never seen anything like this at this school in its history, 17 years, never had someone come in and be able to connect to our students and command respect like he did.' It was remarkable watching about 1,100 students with their eyes on him for 40 minutes. That's hard for a high school kid to do. The other thing that happens, we have had to change the amount of speaking time to accommodate for students wanting to interact with him. So many students want to high-five him, shake his hand, get a picture with him, that we had to change how we were doing things because it was so impactful."

His speaking career got off to an inauspicious start, but not because of anything he said or did. On his way to Colorado the first visit to Billings' school district, the airline lost his luggage. Timothy landed in Denver; all of his belongings—including the several medications he is required to take every day to manage his body—landed in Dallas. He got to his hotel around 2:30 a.m., with a full day of speaking to come early in the morning.

What unfolded convinced Billings that he had met a special man.

"They lost all his luggage; all of his medical needs are in his luggage," Billings remembered. "Having not spent much time around people who are in a wheelchair, there was no way for me to appreciate how significant that was. But he was calm, not dejected, not upset. We took it all in stride, we exhausted every way to find his luggage and finally were told by airline they believed his luggage was in Dallas and the best hope is that it would come the next day.

"His resolve was just 'matter-of-fact, we'll deal with it and it'll be fine.' But learning after the fact what it meant for him and the impact it had, I would say 99.9 percent of the population would have come undone, but not Timothy. What he did was just remarkable. I don't know other words to use. He went on to speak in Greeley by mid-morning, he didn't have his medicine —his most essential items—and never once did he even suggest that he might not be able to speak. He went

Photo courtesy of Bob Billings

Students at Northridge High School in Colorado are captivated by Timothy Alexander's message. Timothy now delivers his motivational message at schools across the nation.

through it and tore it up.

"People were in tears and he just did an incredible job. It goes without saying he's like nobody I have ever known in his resolve to be great."

Timothy had another goal for that first Colorado trip: He wanted to go skiing.

The trip organizers set up an opportunity for Timothy but upon arrival it was learned that Timothy —at 6 foot 5, 260 pounds—was much too large for the facilities that enabled handicapped access at the ski slope.

"In my two-plus years of knowing him, that young man does not take no for an answer," Billings recalled. Billings lined up the next best thing. Before he left Colorado, Timothy Alexander was driving a snowmobile through the white snow of the Rocky Mountains, all the way to the Continental Divide.

As he looks at the photos today, Bob Billings just marvels at Timothy's journey. A young man from the streets of Birmingham, Ala., had come so far and he was taking so many along for the ride.

"He seems totally at ease," Billings recalled. "That's one of the things that quite frankly is amazing, whether it is something brand new or something he's done many times, he makes it seem like it's no big deal and he's got it handled. …

"It was a God thing that put us at those two tables. There was a reason we were seated next to each other and that we have continued to see each other. Did I ever think I would be in circumstance to have a great

Photo courtesy of Bob Billings

A speaking engagement in Colorado took Timothy Alexander to the Continental Divide via snowmobile.

friend and amazing man as part of my life? Not in a hundred years. It was meant to be."

Timothy is at his best when he is working with children.

"Tim around kids is the funniest thing to see," his teammate, Tristan Henderson said. "You like to joke around with him because of the light he brings to everything. One thing in everything he does, he wants those kids to have a memory. Everything he does around kids, regardless of whether they are joking, or playing, or throwing a football around, he gives them a memory of something. He gives them that thought of, 'Remember when Mr. Alexander said this.' It plays in their minds."

One of the best moments led to one of the remarkable events of the 2017 UAB season. As the team's Director of Character Development, Timothy looked for ways for the football program to give back to the community through service. A partnership was created with Children's Harbor, a charity that provides family services for patients at the nearby Children's Hospital. The team wore special patches on special uniforms for their homecoming game against Louisiana Tech. On the backs of their jerseys, players wore the names of children from the hospital instead of their own.

It held special meaning for Timothy because of a special relationship he held with a former patient. Emmy Nichols, young daughter of one of the original UAB football players, was diagnosed with a benign brain tumor. Before she was taken to surgery, a call was made to Timothy. He didn't know what the call was about, "but when they call me, I go," he said. Emmy wanted to meet the man she had seen on television. Timothy learned the seriousness of her surgery. In the hospital room, they prayed. Emmy said she was afraid to die.

"When she came to, she wrote me a letter," he said. "It said, 'Because you came to see me, it gave me hope to live my life.'

"That's one of the things that inspires me, to be a role model and to inspire people beyond their tragedies and adversities, the hardships that they are going through. To let them know I overcame mine, and you can overcome yours."

The Blazers were mightily inspired that game,

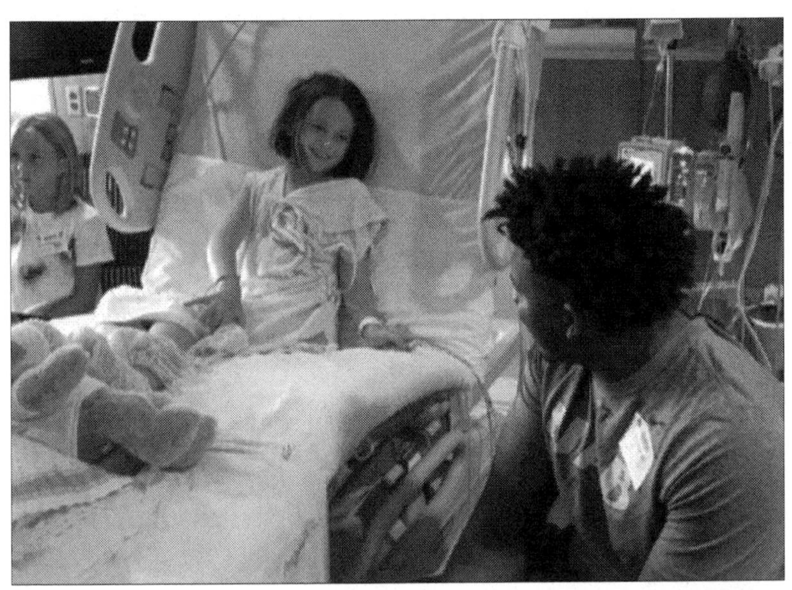

Photo courtesy of William Nichols

Timothy took time to speak to Emmy Nichols from her hospital bed before her brain surgery.

too. With team captain Shaq Jones wearing Emmy's name on the back of his No. 42 jersey, the Blazers blocked a field goal on the last play and upset favored Louisiana Tech 25-23 on Homecoming.

"People may look at me and say, 'that young man in that wheelchair, he's done this and this and this,'" Timothy said. "But how did he do it? It's because he cast his vision. And he went after it every single day. In 2006, my house burned down. I lost my brother. I had a horrific car accident. My back was up against the wall and that's when I pressed in. Was I suicidal? Yes. Did I try to take my life? Absolutely. But after you've endured so much, there's only one thing left to do and that's keep moving forward. My life is a life of resilience, consistency and persistence."

What else might Timothy accomplish with his life? Friends are almost universal in their assessment:

"The sky is the limit for Tim," said Jordan Howard, the Chicago Bears running back.

"Anything he wants to do," Henderson said. "That guy is smart, charismatic, knows what he wants and he goes after it. That's just Tim. Anything he wants to do, he's going to do it. Tim wants to walk? I'm pretty sure he's going to walk."

Timothy is certain of that. The ten yards he covered to midfield for the return of UAB football was just a start. Kayla Bryant, he promised, would be walked down the aisle when she becomes Mrs. Timothy Alexander.

18

Chapter

Paradise Found

Nassau, Bahamas was a fitting destination for the final game of the 2017 UAB football season. As he basked in the sunshine of an island paradise, Timothy Alexander reflected back on the journey.

Remember, he predicted it all. When everyone told him UAB football was dead, he said it would return. When Las Vegas oddsmakers set the over-under for Blazer victories at 2.5 in their inaugural season back, Timothy told anyone who would listen that the Blazers would be bowl-eligible. When Marty Smith of ESPN, via video message on the scoreboard at Bartow Arena, revealed the destination, cheers went up. The Blazers, winners of eight games —including a perfect 6-0 at Legion Field in Birmingham—would face the Ohio University Bobcats in the Bahamas Bowl.

The local television cameras turned to Timothy, who knew what the oddsmakers didn't.

"Remember, it's not what you go through, it's what you grow through," he said and then repeated. Timothy Alexander had grown so much.

Dr. Ray Watts, who had made the decision to kill the UAB football, bowling and rifle programs, now could be seen at Blazer games at one of their biggest cheerleaders. He spearheaded the fund-raising efforts, working with the newly established UAB Athletics Foundation, and worked behind the scenes with civic leaders as Birmingham attempted to secure funding for

Photo courtesy of Patricia Alexander

Doctors at one time believed Timothy Alexander's brain damage from an automobile accident might prevent him from reading, writing or even speaking again. Instead he earned two bachelor's degrees, a master's degree and plans to pursue a doctorate.

a new $174 million, 45,000-seat stadium at the city's Uptown entertainment district. He also locked up his football coach, Bill Clark, with a contract extention. In the fall of 2017, UAB enrolled the largest freshman class in its history and set an overall enrollment record for the second consecutive year to approach 21,000 students.

Without question, the energy created by the return of the programs played a role in it.

"Our consistent enrollment growth across the board is a result of, and a testament to, the dedication of all UAB students, faculty and staff, as well as our many supporters in Birmingham, Alabama, and beyond," Watts said in a release. "There is a growing energy and excitement on campus—momentum that represents many people working with strategic focus toward UAB's standards of excellence in education, research, community service and economic development."

This was the message Timothy had preached all along: Bringing back the programs would unite the community around the university and unite the university to the community.

Speaking to a group of business leaders at a Hoover Chamber of Commerce luncheon, athletic director Mark Ingram re-told the story of The Return. After the groundswell of support generated by Timothy and his band of Free UAB warriors, the business community—led by a key group of boosters that UAB came to know as the "Gang of Seven," stepped in to fill the financial gap. The meeting was in late May 2015, as Watts was moving toward a final decision on the programs.

"This guy on the back wall stands up and he says, 'You know Dr. Watts, I'm not really a sports fan. I don't think I've ever been to a football game at UAB. I think maybe I've been to two basketball games. But I've seen what this has done to our community and we've got to fix this. I'm in for a million.' And this guy doesn't even go to our games!"

Around the room they went, with pledges being kicked in. Another million. Another million. A half-million. By the end of the meeting, there was a feeling UAB football—and bowling and rifle—were soon to be back.

"That's the kind of support we needed," Ingram said. "As odd as it is, losing it was the best thing that ever happened because people realized how important it was to the community.

There are diehard UAB supporters who would dispute the idea that their programs had to be killed in

Photo courtesy of Timothy Alexander

With his campaign to restore the UAB football, bowling and rifle programs completed, Timothy Alexander is all smiles as he poses for a photo with UAB President Ray Watts, the man who killed and then reinstated them.

order to live, but the end result was magnificent.

As he soaked in the fruits of his labor in the Bahamas, Timothy was already thinking about his biggest goal of all: He is determined to walk again—without the support of braces. No one close to him doubts they will see it happen.

"He still has that drive to this day," said Natalie Shannon, Timothy's physical therapist at Drayer Physical Therapy. "That is probably one of the most incredible things, seeing what he is willing to put into his therapy and workouts outside of therapy."

Said Bob Billings, the education administrator from Colorado: "When he says he is going to do something, I'm not doubting. If I am betting, I am putting my money on Tim Alexander."

Former Blazer football player Tristan Henderson can't wait for that day.

"Tim will walk again. I have no doubt that man will walk again," said Henderson, the man who stood up to Watts in the meeting where the football program was killed and who, as a fellow tight end, was among his closest friends on the football team. "I've already told him that when he does, I am going to knock him on his butt," he added with a laugh.

It all ties in to Timothy's catch phrase, the one he says at every speaking engagement. Living these words carried him through the darkest times as he fought for his life, and later fought to save the program that represented all his hopes and dreams. It is the phrase that has marked his transformation from juvenile offender to two-time college graduate on his way to earning a doctorate in Diversity Development. It describes his path from paralyzed football player in a wheelchair to man walking to midfield at a college football game. It marks his rise from the streets of Center Point, Alabama, to world traveler who has mingled with millionaires, driven a snowmobile to the Continental Divide, felt the breeze of the Pacific on his face in Malibu, California, and this week planned to swim with sharks in the Atlantic.

"We don't need it to be easy," Timothy Alexander will tell you. "We just need it to be possible."

Timothy Alexander greets members of the 2017 UAB football team as they prepare to take the field to face Ohio University in the Bahamas Bowl. Timothy correctly predicted the Blazers would be bowl-eligible in their first season back.

ABOUT THE AUTHORS

Tim Stephens

Fort Payne, Ala., native Tim Stephens has led some of the nation's most innovative news organizations into the digital age during a media career that began as a sports reporter at his hometown newspaper while still in high school. As Vice President at SportsManias, Stephens helped a startup company become the fastest-growing sports news app in the United States.

Before joining SportsManias, Stephens led news organizations that captured journalism and broadcast awards and pioneered digital and social-media strategy. He served as Deputy Managing Editor at CBSSports.com and sports editor of the Orlando Sentinel, South Florida Sun-Sentinel and Birmingham Post-Herald, where he was named the nation's top sports columnist in 2003 in the newspaper's circulation division. Stephens was elected president of the Associated Press Sports Editors in 2013-14. He is a graduate of the University of Alabama at Birmingham and active lifetime member of the UAB National Alumni Society as well as a two-time winner of the UAB Excellence in Business Top 25 award. In 2017, he was elected to the alumni board of the UAB College of

Arts and Sciences.

Stephens also has served as a sports talk-show host on WJOX 690 AM and WERC 960 AM in Birmingham and WQTM 740 AM in Orlando and was the color analyst for broadcasts of UAB football games from 1993-95. He is founder and CEO of Tim Stephens Media LLC, providing consulting and services in publishing, digital content marketing and strategic communications.

"Ever Faithful, Ever Loyal: The Timothy Alexander Story" is his first book.

*** *** ***

Timothy Alexander

A native of Birmingham, Ala., Timothy Alexander is a devout Christian, motivational speaker and life coach. As a senior at E.B. Erwin High School in 2006, Timothy was one of the state's top-ranked football players. However, he was involved in a life-changing car accident that fall, leaving him paralyzed from the neck down. From that point on, Timothy was left to find his purpose in life while paralyzed.

Timothy graduated from Erwin in 2007 and attended Wallace State Community College. After graduating from Wallace State, he enrolled at The University of Alabama at Birmingham, where he double majored in Criminal Justice and Communication Management. While at UAB, Timothy earned a football scholarship with the Blazers despite being a paraplegic. He was runner-up for the Mr. UAB Award, a member of Omega Psi Phi fraternity and president of the UAB Gang Green student spirit club.

When UAB terminated its football, bowling and rifle programs on Dec. 2, 2014, Timothy led a grassroots movement to protest the decision. After receiving more than 50 city and county proclamations supporting the reinstatement of the three teams, he joined with UAB boosters and Birmingham city leaders to help raise more than $40 million in one year as the university restored the programs. Timothy graduated from UAB with a Master's degree in Communication Management. His proudest moment came on July 18, 2016 when he was able to stand up on his own for the first time since being paralyzed. In January 2017, Timothy received an Emmy Award for his work on a television special about the UAB football saga.

Timothy is also a minister, keynote speaker and graduate of the John C. Maxwell Certification Program.

THANK YOU

Timothy Alexander's story is one of the most inspiring I've encountered in 30 years as a professional journalist, but helping him share it with the world was a team effort.

First off, thank you Timothy, his family and friends for sharing their time, memories and photos for multiple interviews throughout the process. Like the writing of the book, his story is group effort, too. Thanks especially to Timothy's mother, Patricia, who never ceases to amaze me with her positive outlook on life.

Thanks to the entire staff at UAB Athletics, to the UAB National Alumni Society and the UAB administration for their patience and cooperation. Thank you, Coach Bill Clark and the entire UAB football team. And especially thank you to the thousands of fans of the Free UAB movement who fought alongside Timothy to bring back the UAB football, bowling and rifle programs. They call this the UAB Family, and it is unlike any other athletics program I have ever seen.

Thank you to the late Gene Bartow, who recruited me to UAB in 1991 and taught me so much about college athletics and leadership. Thank you to the many writers and editors who have inspired and mentored me over the years, a list that includes but is not limited to: Joey Bunch, Don Kausler Jr., Lynn Hoppes, the late Clarke Stallworth and the late, great Van McKenzie.

Thank you to Tom Brew and Hilltop30 Publishing. Tom is a great friend and trusted editor who helped make this project better in every way.

Thank you to the people closest to me who encouraged me along the way. You know who you are. I love you.

Lastly, thank you my mother and father, who never stopped believing in me. Dad has battled cancer while I worked on this project and encouraged me throughout during a time when I was trying to encourage him. But that's my dad, the most selfless man I have ever known. He is my hero.

– Tim Stephens

First of all, thank you to my Lord and Savior Jesus Christ, through Him all things are possible. Thank you also to my spiritual father, Bishop Stephen A. Davis and Bishop Eddie L. Long, for speaking into my life.

Thank you Mr. Phillips and Coach Willie Miller, for seeing potential in me at Erwin High School and challenging me to give my best.

Thank you to my family and particularly my Mom for all you've done for me. Thank you to Kayla Bryant, the love of my life. I love you. Thanks for all your support and pushing me to be better than I was yesterday.

Thank you to Coach Garrick McGee for putting me on the football team at UAB and thank you Coach Bill Clark for the opportunity to grow first in my role as a teammate and now as a character coach. Thank you Brian Mackin, former athletic director of the University of Alabama at Birmingham, for supporting my involvement as a student-athlete in our institution. Thank you to former UAB strength coach Zac Woodfin for a moment at the top of Legion Field that changed my life forever. Thank you

Coach Richard Owens for believing in me and allowing me to be a tight end for the UAB Blazers and making it possible for me to contribute to our team.

Thank you to UAB athletic trainer Mike Jones and the entire staff at Drayer Physical Therapy for helping me find my strength again. Thank you Justin Craft and the entire Free UAB Movement for being a living example of "Ever-faithful Ever-loyal." We did it! Thank you Phyllis Rogers, Kris Findlay, and Thanasis Nicolau. I'll never forget that "No is not a option!"

Thank you, Cynthia Murphy, Yolanda Spencer and Alabama Vocational Rehabilitation Services for showing me that my disability is only an ability to to achieve my maximum potential.

Thank you to the greatest fraternity on this side of heaven, Omega Psi Phi, for pushing me to live out our four cardinal principles: Manhood, Scholarship, Perseverance and Uplift daily!

Lastly, thank you Growing Leaders and the rest of my support team for allowing me to share my story all over the world.

To get more information on book signings and speaking engagements, or to find out how to book Timothy Alexander as a speaker at your next event, visit InspiredByTA.com. Be sure to follow the continuing journey on Twitter, Facebook and Instagram (@inspiredbyTA). And remember: "We don't need it to be easy, we just need it to be possible."

– Timothy Alexander

WHAT THEY'RE SAYING

"Timothy Alexander never ceases to amaze me with his tenacity, drive and ability to get things done with a smile on his face. If you need to be in the presence of a good human being that will redeem your faith in humanity, he's the person."

— Rachel Baribeau,
SiriusXM College Sports Nation host

*** *** ***

"There aren't enough words to describe Timothy Alexander. He is somebody that when you see him, you just want to drop everything and give him a hug. You want to embrace him because he embraces life like nobody I have ever seen before or anybody I have ever met. He has taken his situation and turned it into something extremely positive and is impacting more people than he will ever know. Throughout this entire journey, he has stayed humble. He is using his circumstance for the greater good. That is one of life's greatest rewards, and he has taught me that."

— Lauren Sisler, AL.com multimedia reporter
and correspondent for the SEC Network

*** *** ***

"(Timothy Alexander) was the face of the return of UAB football. ... I really believe people saw his perseverance and determination and it was translated into a group that wasn't going to take no for an answer. They said, 'We're going to get our football program back.' People listened. Timothy could be the guy that everyone points to in the future, saying, 'without him we may have been able to get it done, but *with* him we absolutely were able to get it done.'"

— Gene Hallman,
Bruno Event Team chairman

*** *** ***

"I love the fact that Timothy Alexander has a servant's heart. I've never heard him say a negative word about anybody. He's is such a very positive person who loves to encourage people. A lot of people in his situation might become bitter and cynical and chronically negative, and he's just the opposite. He's the kind of guy we need to represent this entire city. He's awesome."

— James Spann, chief meteorologist,
Birmingham's ABC 33/40

*** *** ***

"Timothy is the epitome of endurance, consistency and strong will to accomplish the things that he sets as his goals and dreams in life. Tim doesn't give up. He believes he can encourage young people, middle-aged people, elderly people, regardless of what arena he is in. He walks in as a light."

— Bishop Stephen A. Davis,
senior pastor, New Life Birmingham

*** *** ***

"Timothy Alexander is the human statue to the success of UAB — a statue with a pulse. Energy and enthusiasm and love and passion resonate with him."

— Tim Brando, broadcaster, Fox Sports